Get Smashed.

Get Smashed.

The story of the men who made the
adverts that changed our lives.

Sam Delaney

SCEPTRE

Copyright © 2007 by Sam Delaney

First published in Great Britain in 2007 by Hodder & Stoughton
A division of Hodder Headline

The right of Sam Delaney to be identified as the Author of
the Work has been asserted by him in accordance with
the Copyright, Designs and Patents Act 1988.

A Sceptre Book

1

A CIP catalogue record for this title is available from the British Library

ISBN 978-0-340-92250 7

Typeset in Futura by Hewer Text UK Ltd, Edinburgh
Printed and bound by Clays Ltd, St Ives plc

Hodder Headline's policy is to use papers that are natural, renewable
and recyclable products and made from wood grown in sustainable
forests. The logging and manufacturing processes are expected to
conform to the environmental regulations of the country of origin.

Hodder & Stoughton Ltd
A division of Hodder Headline
338 Euston Road
London NW1 3BH

For Anna

Contents

Introduction

In the early seventies, Cadbury's commissioned the advertising agency Boase Massimi Pollitt to make an advert for their instant mash potato brand. Gray Jolliffe, one of the agency's writers, remembers his managing director walking in with the brief.

He said, 'We need a little jingle to go at the end of these ads. Can anyone think of one?' I said, 'What's the name of the product?' and he said, 'Smash.' So I said, 'What about "For Mash Get Smash?"' He wrote it down on a piece of paper, said thanks, and walked out again. Now, the cleaning lady could have come up with the same line. It was the most obvious thing in the world. But for the rest of my career people would say 'Oh, there's Gray Jolliffe. He's famous because he wrote "For Mash Get Smash".' I'm not proud of it, I'm just embarrassed by anyone thinking that it's important.

In advertising, that sort of thing really is important. A throwaway line has the potential to make millions of pounds for a company – and make the career of its creator. An industry in which people are credited with genius for conjuring catchy rhymes, writing simple puns or inventing cuddly characters to promote breakfast cereals can seem a bit silly from the outside.

Between the 1960s and the 1980s, the British advertising industry was at its silliest. This was a time in which social, political and cultural forces aligned to transform an industry that had once been dull and uninspiring into a hotbed of creativity. For the first time, advertising was thrust to the forefront of the British public's consciousness, as a new generation of admen revolutionised the business. They drank, they fought, they took drugs and they bedded women as if they were rock stars. All in the name of making thirty-second adverts for everyday consumer products. They convinced themselves that what they were doing was more than just selling; they thought it was art. During this brief period, a multimillion-pound industry previously run by upright public schoolboys and ex-army officers was taken over by a bizarre menagerie of interlopers: from hare-brained American heroin addicts to Bosnian Nazi assassins, they swaggered into the head offices of corporate Britain and told them how to sell their products. And charged them a fortune for it. 'For while, we had all the power,' says a leading figure of the times. 'The lunatics had taken over the asylum.'

Much of this unique generation of men had come and gone within the space of twenty-five years. In the interim, they created some of the most memorable ads of all time: from the Smash Martians to the Honeymonster to the Levi's launderette. Many of those responsible had joined the industry as raw, uneducated hoodlums. But advertising had made most of them millionaires by the time they were thirty. The strangest thing about this story is the sheer weight of talent that seemed to arrive in advertising at exactly the same time, purely by chance. Ridley Scott, Alan Parker, Charles Saatchi, David Puttnam, Peter Mayle, Hugh Hudson and Adrian Lyne: these are the men who worked their way up through Britain's advertising agencies and changed the business for ever. Soon, they had left to become film-makers, art dealers, novelists or politicians. The industry grew up and became sensible again. Great ads continued to be made but never again would they be made in the same heady climate of passion, chaos and hedonistic abandon. What follows is a snapshot of those times.

1

'Think Small'

In 1954, the idea of television advertisements was still a strange and confusing one to British businesses. In those simpler times, TV itself was still considered to be borderline witchcraft; the thought of people accepting grubby salesmen into their living rooms every night seemed quite preposterous. To help would-be advertisers get to grips with this vulgar notion, a helpful pamphlet was produced by Alfred Pemberton Limited's TV, Film and Radio Division. It was entitled *Television Advertising* and methodically explained the advantages of this fanciful new medium. 'Like cinema but with the added strength of being viewed in one's own home,' it explained. 'Television offers sales impact through the combined effect of sound, image, motion and animated lettering.' It was a convincing argument. The pamphlet even made persuasive suggestions as to the content of commercials. 'Factual portrayals of doings, happenings, places or things' were highly recommended. Even the costs of such promotional films were said to be modest: 'Production costs of a filmed one-minute commercial run from about £200 for a straight sales talk to about £2,000 for complete animation accompanied by voices, music, sound effects and a good jingle. Average costs of a single commercial run at about £500, but . . . nearly half of this can be saved by careful planning.' The pamphlet aimed to take the fear out of television advertising. It made it all sound so simple. And it could have been, if only someone had remembered the bit about careful planning.

By 1997, there were few corners of the world that hadn't been touched by the extravagant force of television advertising. By then, people living in every region of the planet had, in one way or another, their perceptions, aspirations and behaviour impacted upon by those supersonic, neon-lit, thirty-second films that punctuated their favourite TV shows. With the exception, that is, of the tribes of Mexico's Oaxaca region. Spreading inland from Mexico's south-west coast, Oaxaca is a territory of unique beauty and culture. It has peaks almost 10,000 feet high, caverns among the deepest in the world, virgin beaches, hidden jungles and luminous valleys that house populations where at least half the people still speak an indigenous dialect.

So they would doubtless have been surprised to see a fifty-strong production team troop into their village carrying an arsenal of cameras and lights on a hot summer's morning. As the crew busied themselves with turning this glorious, untainted hamlet into a fully functioning film set, the producer demanded to speak to the tribal chief. The chief emerged from his hut wearing little but an expression of anger and confusion. He demanded an explanation for this imposition. With all the confidence of a man who considered himself to be above anyone's law but his own, the British producer turned to his interpreter and said, 'Tell him we're from London. Tell him we have money. Tell him we're here to make a commercial!'

The film crew was in the employ of Abbott Meade Vickers, one of London's most successful and fashionable advertising agencies.

They had been in Mexico for two weeks making a commercial for Delta Airlines. Such was their need to shoot in a number of different locations across the vast country, they'd decided to hire their own private plane. But the only aircraft capable of accommodating them and their equipment was the Hercules that belonged to the Mexican postal service. They'd hired it complete with pilots, strapped in a number of seats and two building-site Portaloos and set off on an airbourne advertising adventure.

The representative sent by the agency to keep an eye on costs was a nervous flyer. In fact, she was so disturbed by the prospect of flying in this jalopy that her colleagues would force-feed her tequila in order to get her on board. During one flight, she woke from her hangover to see a junior member of the production team at the controls, banking the plane fiercely across the skies in fits of giggles. After the screams had faded, the production manager got up and made an earnest announcement to his boisterous team of cohorts: 'From now on, no one is to fly this plane other than the pilots!'

The crew eventually arrived in Oaxaca in pursuit of one last, magnificent shot of the region's sweeping vistas. Their village destination was, according to the commercial's co-directors, the only place from which this image could be captured. 'How much do you want?' the producer asked the tribal chief. 'Money is meaningless to us,' he explained to the interpreter. 'You might as well hand us a bag full of leaves!' But like every other seasoned ad executive on earth, the producer knew that every man has his price. 'If money's no good, then what else might be of value to your village?' The chief thought long and hard before responding. 'A dentist! The whole village is in pain. We need someone to come and fix our teeth.' A call was made via satellite phone to Mexico City. Within two hours, the capital's top dental practitioner was arriving by helicopter in Oaxaca. And while he treated the dental complaints of a hundred tribespeople at one end of the village, the men from London's adland completed their commercial a few yards away. It had taken several weeks, miles of travelling and a million pounds to make. The

Mexican postal service would take six weeks to catch up with the backlog caused by the temporary loss of their plane. But at least Delta would now have a fantastic advert with which to grace UK television screens. Only it never did. A week after the crew had finished their production, Delta appointed a new marketing director. He immediately put a freeze on all work that had been commissioned by his predecessor. He wanted to change the direction of Delta's advertising and so, ultimately, the ad was canned. All that was left to show for the airline's massive outlay was a smiling tribe with the best teeth in Oaxaca.

Television advertising had spiralled far beyond the wildest dreams of Arthur Pemberton Limited. By the end of the twentieth century, ad production teams rolled into exotic locations across the globe like the US military mixed with Zippy's Circus. Fuelled by gargantuan sums of money and their own sense of self-importance, they operated like independent states. The values of those they encountered were insignificant compared to the important nature of their work. Nothing was allowed to stand between them and the successful completion of their adverts. They weren't really to blame for their impertinent attitude. Big business had demanded the best – and their immense financial outlay on advertising was a reflection of the importance they placed upon it. But big business wasn't to blame either. Their faith in the value of advertising, of its ability to generate vast returns and imprint brands into the consciousness of the consumer, had been cultivated many years beforehand. Not by figures, statistics or research. But by the determined vision of one small, quiet man from New York called Bill Bernbach.

Bill Bernbach was the antithesis of what everyone perceived the flashy New York adman to be. For years, Hollywood had portrayed the occupants of Madison Avenue's ad agency sector as cocktail-swilling show-offs in snazzy suits. Clark Gable embodied the species perfectly in the 1947 movie *The Hucksters*. His good looks, smart offices and preoccupation with bedding women seemed to neatly encapsulate the life of an ad executive. Indeed, such trappings were considered to be the very *raison d'être* of the creed. Heaven forbid they should ever aspire to a grander calling than knocking out a snappy slogan in the morning before setting off for that day's decadent lunch appointment. The prevailing advertising theory of the times was neatly expressed by Gable's boss: 'Beauty Soap, Beauty Soap, Beauty Soap! Repeat it till it comes out of their ears. Repeat it till they say it in their sleep. Irritate them . . . irritate, irritate, irritate till they never forget it, then knock them dead.'

Hollywood's perception of the advertising industry was largely accurate. 'Until the fifties, there was no emphasis on advertising's creative side,' says Bob Cooperman of Doyle Dane Bernbach in New York.

> It was run by WASPs who spent their time glad-handing clients over two martinis at the golf course. It was what we called the Good Old Boys' Club. The creative department came way below these guys in terms of importance. The way we made ads was, a writer would come up with some text, then hand it to what we called a visualiser in a separate office. He would draw a picture to go with it and then hand the whole thing over to the account guy whose job it was to convince the client it was worth buying. That was the key.

Movies like *The Hucksters* drew a generation of university graduates into the advertising industry for a taste of the Clark Gable lifestyle. Old-fashioned, behemoth agencies such as McCann-Erickson, Ted Bates, J Walter Thompson and Grey offered it to them. But this did little to attract any employees with genuinely creative ambitions. In the eyes of the wider world, the advertising industry lacked credibility. 'I started out at Ted Bates,' says Cooperman. 'The rule for writers there was: "It doesn't really matter what you're saying as long as you just keep saying it." ' This attitude created an environment of aggressive, gimmicky advertising that assaulted, rather than engaged, the consumer consciousness. Alka Seltzer was endorsed by Speedy, the squeaky-voiced disc with bulging eyes. Animated hammers pounding at a human brain reflected Anadin's painkilling credentials. Lucky Strike's adverts showed its cigarettes dancing across a television screen. Adverts were designed not so much to enchant viewers as harass them into submission.

But advertising's giants insisted that their work got results. They pointed to their sophisticated methodology and scientific research practices as evidence. And while their clients accepted their claims – which they invariably did – the agencies saw no reason to change. Until Bernbach came along. He questioned the authenticity of this supposedly scientific approach; in fact, he dismissed it, proposing that it resulted in dull, repetitive and inane advertising. Worse, he said it didn't work. He was a mine of compelling maxims on the subject: 'I warn you against believing that advertising is a science,' he said. 'Rules are what the artist breaks; the memorable never emerged from a formula,' he added. 'Bill suggested that once you'd worked out what you wanted to say, it was just as important to work out how you should say it,' says Cooperman, who – along with a drove of other frustrated ad makers driven mad by the constrictive methods of the old agencies – flocked to work for Bernbach.

For a man who changed the very nature of advertising, Bernbach's arrival in the industry was unremarkable. 'It just gradually happened,' he said. 'I was interested in writing. I was interested in art, and when the opportunity came along to do writing and art in advertising, I just took the opportunity.' Raised in the Bronx, Bernbach had graduated from New York University in 1932 and found a job in the mailroom at Schenley Distillers. There, he worked closely with Grover Whalen, the company chairman. When Whalen moved on to oversee the 1939 New York World's Fair, Bernbach went with him, becoming his chief speechwriter. He also wrote speeches for governors and mayors. As a result, the young Bernbach spent a great deal of time thinking seriously about how best the English language could be used to persuade the discerning citizen.

These were the days when American people treated politics with more seriousness than consumerism. They wanted more in return for their vote than just a snappy catchphrase. Bernbach identified the importance of speaking to mass audiences with a certain intellectual respect.

Eventually, he transferred his writing talents to advertising with a job at the William Weintraub agency. There, he met the art director Paul Rand. In an era when writers would generally look down their noses at designers, Bernbach was fascinated by Rand's abilities. The two analysed at length how the written word could best be fused with design. By thinking in these collaborative terms, Bernbach was convinced that he could not only improve the commercial effectiveness of advertising but also ennoble its cultural impact. 'All of us who professionally use the mass media are the shapers of society,' he said. 'We can vulgarise that society. We can brutalise it. Or we can help lift it on to a higher level.' His passion for his craft eventually led him away from Weintraub and to the helm of Grey Advertising. There, as creative director, he teamed star art director Bob Gage with copywriting protégée Phyllis Robinson. 'Traditional advertising was so formal,' says Robinson. 'But Bill put us in teams and it made the whole atmosphere so much more relaxed. We would work ideas back and forth until they were perfect. The results were ads that felt friendlier. And people responded to them like crazy.'

Bernbach concluded that his radical approach couldn't fully flourish at an agency the size of Grey. He sent a letter of resignation to the company's directors which read: 'I'm worried . . . that we're going to worship techniques instead of substance. Advertising is fundamentally persuasion and persuasion happens to be not a science, but an art.' Teaming up with account supervisor Ned Doyle and associate Maxwell Dane, he opened Doyle Dane Bernbach at 350 Madison Avenue in 1949. He took his creative stars, Gage and Robinson, with him. 'It just took off like a rocket!' says Robinson of the agency's early successes. 'Grey had been pleasant but the bosses were a little distant. DDB was lively. It was dominated by

New York people and that generated a certain atmosphere. The ads were lively and colloquial.'

Bernbach rejected the 'old boys' club' personnel of the larger agencies. He voiced his concern about their conventional thinking when he said: '. . . they learn the arithmetic of advertising. Now, that very fact that they learn the knowledge of advertising, and the arithmetic of advertising, will work against them as a judge of an ad. You're right, all your facts are right, but you're still dull, because you're saying everything that everybody else is saying.'

Instead, he assembled a maverick team of wisecracking New Yorkers from largely Jewish and Italian backgrounds. Their distinctive tone was reflected in the agency's earliest ads. 'I found out about Joan,' winked a headline on an early print ad for the department store Orbachs. Beside it sat a picture of a cat wearing an oversized hat and smoking from a lengthy cigarette holder. Running beneath was a gossipy housewife's first-person account of how her neighbour could afford to look glamorous only by picking up bargains at the store. It was warm, funny and authentic. No one had read an ad like it before.

Next came Levy's, a small Jewish bakery for whom Bernbach created a slogan of striking simplicity: 'You don't have to be Jewish to love Levy's.' The ads featured people from diverse ethnic backgrounds, including a Native American, enjoying sandwiches made on Levy's rye bread. The campaign quickly broadened the appeal of the struggling bakery and profits rose. Suddenly, it became apparent that, with cleverly crafted ideas, Doyle Dane Bernbach could generate more results for a small client with a paltry budget than a big agency might achieve with a huge, multimillion-dollar account. As their client list grew, DDB continued to confront the public with imagery and language that set the tone for a more liberal post-war America. 'For most people, stability was the goal after the war,' says Bob Cooperman.

But as we moved towards the sixties, consumerism grew and people's aspirations changed. Previously, there was a false premise that if advertising talked to people in their own language then it wouldn't give them anything to aspire to. Bernbach thought they were smart enough to buy into the humour and personality of the ads. Likeability was the key.

Doyle Dane Bernbach's first day of business was day one of the modern advertising age. Their hiring policy was a reflection of their disdain for everything that had gone before them. 'When people came to show me their portfolios, I would always ask to see what was in the back of the book,' says Robinson. 'That was usually the stuff that had been rejected by the bosses at their current agency. Which usually meant it was the good stuff.'

They were inundated with prospective employees. 'Bill used to joke: "They're climbing through the windows!" because we had so many people trying to work for us,' says Robinson.

> Novelists would come and say, 'Is there some way you could make use of me?' One day, a young, blond-haired designer came in and showed me his illustrations. I thought it was interesting but we didn't have any jobs for him. A week later, I saw one of the same illustrations published in the corner of the newspaper, signed Andy Warhol. I thought to myself, 'Bully for him – he made a good start!'

The agency embarked on an uncompromising crusade to revolution-ise the entire industry. They rejected the prevailing culture of paying lip-service to clients. 'We don't permit any client to give us ground rules,' said Bernbach. 'Let me put it this way. We think we will never know as much about a product as a client. After all, he sleeps and breathes his product . . . By the same token, we firmly believe that he can't know as much about advertising. Because *we* live and breathe *that* all day long.' This overriding sense of confidence allowed DDB to successfully overhaul the master-and-servant relationship that had previously existed. It was more than just rhetoric: 'A very, very big prospect once said to me, "What would you say, Bill, if you were told exactly where to put the logo and what size it would be [on an advertisement]?" ' Bernbach revealed. 'I had ten million dollars riding on my answer and I said, "I would say we were the wrong agency for you." '

Never before had the American advertising industry witnessed a company with any agenda other than the accumulation of profit. Doyle Dane Bernbach's refusal to handle cigarette advertising (one of the most lucrative sectors at the time) was considered insane by other agencies. In 1964 they handled Lyndon Johnson's presidential campaign. 'I fundamentally believe that what you think about something affects your writing,' Bernbach explained. 'You know, we had the Johnson campaign because we believe; we would not have taken the opposite side. No matter how much money was involved, we would not have taken it.'

The campaign's high point was a TV advert entitled 'Daisy'. It featured a young girl picking the petals from a flower and ended with a terrifying nuclear explosion. Johnson's rival candidate, Senator Barry Goldwater, was widely thought to be dangerously aggressive in his attitudes towards the Soviet Union. The ad never used Goldwater's name or image, yet the message was clear: Goldwater might use atomic weapons. The ad ran once, on 7 September 1964, during NBC's *Monday Night Movie*. Johnson had to pull the ad after the Republicans complained, but the following night all three network news broadcasts showed the ad in its entirety. 'Nobody counts the number of ads you run,' Bernbach pointed out. 'They just remember the impression you make.'

Doyle Dane Bernbach's greatest creative triumph was their work for Volkswagen. When the German car manufacturer first appeared in the United States, it was anathema to the American car buyer. With the war still fresh in the memory, any German product would have struggled. But the Volkswagen Beetle's small, ugly appearance served as a further hindrance. American citizens liked their cars big, dynamic and manufactured in Detroit. But Bernbach identified a virtue in the Beetle's traits. He appealed to people's intelligence by writing ads that celebrated its unconventional nature. He penned a press ad with the headline 'Think Small'. The proposition was outrageously counter-intuitive. It was the first campaign to be based on a self-deprecating premise, encouraging consumers to 'think small' in terms of price and petrol consumption. The design was in further contrast to traditional car ads. Its bold photographic image, white background, stark black headline and neat blocks of copy looked fresh and sleek. This understated look became a DDB trademark and remained an iconic template for press advertising across the globe for decades. The self-effacing campaign thrived: a subsequent press ad featured a Beetle under the headline 'Lemon'. It confessed that Volkswagen occasionally made a faulty vehicle – but that such a car would always remain on the production line.

In 1963, they successfully moved the campaign to television. Their first commercial featured a man driving through a deep blizzard in his Beetle. Eventually, he arrived at the depot where the county snowploughs were kept. The voice-over then asked, 'Have you ever wondered how the man who drives a snowplough . . . drives to the snowplough? This one drives a Volkswagen. So you can stop wondering.' Years later, DDB's work for Volkswagen was voted the greatest campaign of all time by *Advertising Age* magazine. It elevated Volkswagen to an unlikely place in the higher echelons of American sales successes and confirmed that Bernbach's thoughtful approach was the way forward for the US advertising industry. 'We became the agency for the underdog brand,' says Cooperman. 'The kind of companies who couldn't break into the top ten in their field came to us. They didn't have the money to launch a massive assault on consumers but they knew that we could provide quality, not quantity, and that it would be just as effective.'

Doyle Dane Bernbach's creative department soon housed an all-star line-up of talent: the likes of George Lois, Mary Wells and Helmut Krone would later go on to forge successful careers away from the agency. But each of them would credit their success to the education they received under Bernbach. He was at the hub of everything, quietly guiding his band of firebrands with a sober assurance. 'He was a small man, quietly spoken, who was friendly but never chummy,' says Robinson. 'He had intense blue eyes and always wore grey suits. He wasn't in the least bit flashy.' He was often described as a square among advertising's heaving throng of hipsters – but the respect he commanded was unrivalled. 'He would talk to us about advertising constantly and critique our work without ever being negative,' says Robinson. 'He was responsible for the thoughtful, simple tone that ran through all of our ads.' Despite his unassuming demeanour, Bernbach was not unaware of his own status in the industry. 'It was always rumoured that he carried a small piece of paper in his jacket pocket with the words "Maybe he's right" written on it,' says Cooperman. 'I always suggested that he had a separate piece in another pocket which read "But he probably isn't".'

Soon, the mantra across the whole of Madison Avenue was 'What would Bill think?' Bernbach's were the only criteria by which creative people wanted to judge their adverts. 'We won numerous awards at DDB,' says Cooperman. 'But none of them meant as much to us as the praise of Mr Bernbach. There was a wall in the agency where "Bill's Picks Of The Week" would be hung. To get your ad up there was the greatest aspiration of every creative in the company.'

By the end of the sixties, DDB was no longer the young upstart of American advertising. It was handling accounts worth hundreds of millions of dollars and competing closely with the traditional giants of the industry. 'New agencies started springing up all over town trying to conform to the Bernbach ethos,' says Bob Brooks, who started his career at Benton and Bowles in New York. 'The old agencies gave up trying to fight his theories and decided to embrace them. But they never did so with much success.'

Soon, Bernbach's ideas would spread farther than Madison Avenue. In the early 1960s, Doyle Dane Bernbach prepared to open a London office – but their regard for British advertising was low. 'We would occasionally receive funny-shaped awards in the post from Europe,' recalls Cooperman. 'But we didn't really know what they were. We were barely aware of agencies in other parts of New York, let alone other parts of the world. As far as we were concerned, Doyle Dane Bernbach was where the universe began and ended.'

When Bill Bernbach died of leukaemia in October 1982, *Harper's Bazaar* magazine wrote that he 'probably had a greater impact on American culture than any of the distinguished writers and artists who have appeared in the pages of *Harper's* during the past 133 years'. In 1963, he was about to have the same impact on Great Britain.

2

'Drinka Pinta Milka Day'

Sid Roberson was late back from lunch again. His employers at Benton and Bowles, one of London's biggest and most respectable advertising agencies, were already weary of this rough-talking young bodybuilder from the mean streets of Tottenham who, somehow, had become a junior designer in their art department. As he swaggered back to his desk at 3 p.m., he was about to confirm their worst fears. The advertisement he'd been working on all morning was missing. He hunted furiously for the work, eventually discovering it on the desk of his boss: the creative director of the agency. 'What are you doing with my layout?' the young designer snarled at his superior. The rest of the department fell into a stunned silence. The creative director peered over his spectacles at Roberson and smiled. 'Well, Roberson, old chap,' he began. 'You were taking rather a long time over lunch so I thought I'd take this away and see if I could help you come up with any ideas.' Roberson glared back at him.

'I've got an idea,' he scowled. 'Why don't you go fuck yourself?' By the time he returned to his desk, he'd been fired.

This sort of thing didn't happen in early-sixties Britain. Young people were supposed to respect their elders. Workers were supposed to respect their bosses. Working-class tearaways were supposed to respect well-spoken gentlemen in suits. Sid Roberson's disregard for these conventions was staggering to those who witnessed it. While he calmly packed up his desk and left Benton and Bowles for good, his colleagues looked on in disbelief.

During the decade that followed the war, the advertising industry had proved a popular destination for ex-army officers looking for lucrative positions of authority. Their militaristic air of gravitas and public school vowels proved popular with the similarly respectable heads of British commerce. It was a cosy and comfortable world where old school ties and lavish lunches kept the wheels of industry turning. In the 1950s, a handful of top agencies handled the vast majority of Britain's biggest-spending companies, offering them the full gamut of marketing services: from package design to market research to poster, press and, eventually, television advertisements.

The purpose of these adverts was to aggressively implant the name of a product into the consumer's mind. Pun-based slogans, catchy jingles and novelty corporate mascots were popular ways of achieving this end. Low prices, higher speeds, bigger sizes and better value were the popular selling points of the time. An agency's overriding preoccupation was to reassure clients that advertising was not a gamble but a science. They even formed an industry group and gave it the grand title of Institute of Practitioners in Advertising. These were people who wanted to be taken seriously. They had a great deal riding on it. Even in the 1950s, British industry was spending millions on advertising. In order to maintain this profitable arrangement, advertising agencies needed to constantly reassure clients that they were dealing with professionals. This was why the suited executives from client relations served as the public face of most agencies. Behind the scenes, it was the role of the research specialists and strategists that

18

was emphasised. Meanwhile, those who actually wrote and designed the advertisements were kept safely out of view.

In most agencies, the 'creative' department was tucked away in the basement. It was typically staffed by frustrated painters, poets and novelists who had been reduced to the vulgar practice of advertising in order to pay the bills. One agency referred to their staff of writers as the 'literary department'. Whatever their titles, they were considered relatively small cogs in a larger wheel. Neither the creatives themselves nor the companies who employed them were particularly keen to highlight their role to the wider world. Clients tended to be disconcerted by the vagaries of the creative mind.

Not that British advertising's formal, businesslike approach hadn't produced some creative successes. Iconic characters such as the Bisto Kids and Nipper the HMV Dog had been popular with the public since long before the war. Agencies were able to show a strong statistical link between advertising expenditure and sales. But little thought was given to the more subtle impact advertising might have on the consumer consciousness. Emphasising anything less than advertising's definite, tangible effects was considered damaging to the industry. Advertising was serious, professional and nononsense. It was an industry of thoroughly decent chaps, pinstriped suits and rigid hierarchies.

That was until the likes of Sid Roberson began to sneak in through the back door. He embodied a new generation of improbable young scallywags who were making the most of greater prosperity and social mobility. They were unimpressed by authority and tradition and wanted to shake up the stuffy atmosphere that had engulfed the British Isles for the past three decades. And they intended to enjoy themselves in the process.

Benton and Bowles was not the first agency to lose patience with Roberson's unconventional personality. He recalled:

I was being sacked all the time. At one place I kept complaining about the poor standard of work we were being encouraged to do. One day the boss walked in and said, 'Do you want to come to a leaving party?' I said, 'Sure, whose is it?' and he said, 'Yours!' Another agency I worked at was run by these two small American guys. Because I had long hair and a working-class accent they accused me of being a communist. As it happened I was but they didn't actually know that. They fired me anyway.

Like many of his contemporaries, Roberson was initially indifferent towards the work. 'I hadn't gone into advertising because of any burning ambition to be creative,' he explains.

I just stumbled into it really. But after a while I met another guy who was from the same sort of background as me. He was working class but he was very enthusiastic about the creative side of the business. He could talk about it without being poncey. He won me over really and encouraged me to go to art school in the evenings.

A whole generation of future advertising stars were stumbling into the industry by default. 'When I left school at seventeen I was offered two jobs,' recalls Frank Lowe, who left his home town of Manchester for London in the late fifties.

One on the *Aberdeen Courier* as a trainee journalist and the other in the dispatch department of J Walter Thompson. I thought, I'm not going to Aberdeen and I'll probably make a lousy journalist. The job at JWT offered me four pounds and five pence per week plus luncheon vouchers so I went to London.

Lowe took up his job at JWT's grand, antique-furnished offices on Berkeley Square with few expectations.

I knew nothing about the industry at all. In those days, British advertising was rubbish and full of boring jingles like 'You'll wonder where the yellow went when you brush your teeth with Pepsodent!' Nobody ever thought, I must get into advertising. The creative people when I started were all Oxford graduates sitting behind typewriters. The account men were all from the army and the secretaries all had double-barrelled names and scarves tied round their heads. Everyone worked there because it was convenient. I worked there because I thought it was the sort of job where you could do a bit of work, have a bit of fun, go out to lunch and then get paid for it.

Advertising agencies had always struggled to attract the best young creative minds. Britain's cultural tradition dictated that to make things was respectable but to sell them was vulgar. Selling, commerce and trade were terms with seedy connotations in a Britain still in its capitalist infancy. London's top art schools enjoyed a renowned reputation in the late fifties but, to their students, the advertising industry was anathema. 'It wasn't an industry that anyone talked about,' says John Webster, who was three years into a painting course at Hornsey Art School when he quit to join an agency. 'If anyone worked in advertising they didn't admit to it. It was kind of a dodgy business which commanded no respect and was altogether grim.' Nonetheless, a two-week placement at Mather and Crowther was enough to make him abandon his dreams of painting. 'I worked with the guy who did all the fashion ads. So every day I was going along to photo shoots with people like David Bailey and Jean Shrimpton. I thought to myself, I love this world, it's so exciting. So I left school and stayed at the agency.' Mather and Crowther had produced several popular slogans of the time such as 'Drinka Pinta Milka Day', 'People Love Players' and 'I'm Going Well, I'm Going Shell'. This was largely the work of an esteemed, if unlikely, copywriting department. 'It was a bit like the Chelsea Arts Club,' recalls Webster. 'The ads were being written by Fay Weldon and Edwin Brock. They were writing quite good stuff but their hearts were elsewhere.' Weldon earned acclaim for penning the slogan 'Go to work an egg' before leaving the industry to become a critically acclaimed writer of plays and bestselling novels. Brock's brief stint in advertising preceded his fame as a successful poet. For a suburban boy like Webster, it was an intimidating atmosphere. 'Everyone spoke very well and it had the feeling of an old-boy network. Regional accents were considered lower class and I felt constantly inferior in the presence of these very clever people.'

Others witnessed this prejudice from the opposite side. David Abbott arrived at Mather and Crowther shortly after Webster. He had left Oxford University a year into his English degree to find a job and the agency was impressed with his sound, middle-class credentials.

> They made me do a copy test to see if I could write properly. They told me I'd failed but gave me another chance because they said they thought I was the right type. Not because I had a fantastic portfolio but because they thought I'd fit in. They saw me as a decent sort of chap, very presentable. At that time, if the industry wasn't like a public school then it was at least like a good grammar.

Those who didn't share Abbott's educational and social background struggled to make it out of agency post rooms. 'I went for an interview at a large agency called Foote, Cone and Belding,' says Alan Parker (who would later become one of Britain's most successful film directors). 'The creative director there was very much of the old school and all the questions he asked were about the last play I saw and the last record I bought. In the end he said, "You're not really the kind of person I would like to socialise with. I couldn't possibly employ anybody who wasn't into jazz."'

American music, European cinema and the burgeoning revolutions in fashion and art had exposed young Brits to a new and exciting world. But institutionalised snobbery still thwarted many of their ambitions. Some industries were resistant to the cultural and social revolution that was bubbling all around them. But most advertising companies soon realised that embracing these changes was their only hope of survival. It was this imperative which would allow the likes of Parker, Roberson, Lowe, Abbott and Webster to change the industry for ever.

'Suddenly, one day, the plates moved,' says David Abbott. 'The only criterion that mattered in the industry was producing great work. And the people who created that work became the new stars.'

During a period of rapid transformation in the early part of the decade, advertising would become the first demonstration of the sixties mentality being applied to business. The cultural snobbery that had initially hindered the likes of Parker gave way to a more meritocratic approach. 'Colin Millward, who hired me as a writer at Collett Dickenson Pearce, had been a star pupil at the Royal College of Art during the same era as David Hockney,' says Parker. 'He had that art school attitude where all that mattered was the standard of the work you produced. Your accent, your qualifications and where you went to school were completely irrelevant.'

A political shift was taking place in Britain which encouraged a more egalitarian culture. 'I think the whole thing started to become easier for people when Harold Wilson came into power,' says John Webster.

We'd had Harold Macmillan for years, who was an old-fashioned sort of prime minister. Then in came this more down-to-earth bloke with a Manchester accent, wearing a mac. It all exploded at the same time. The Beatles, Mary Quant, David Hockney and Michael Caine all came to prominence. All of a sudden it felt as if having a posh accent was a hindrance. It was the birth of the 'upper-class twit' as comic character.

This fast-changing atmosphere had a deep and immediate impact on the advertising industry. Maintaining a chummy relationship with clients was no longer enough to preserve business. Economic growth had created a new wave of consumerism in which young people possessed disposable income for the first time. In order to make the most of this fresh market, big business needed to make sense of the new culture from which it was born. This was a difficult task for the elderly and confused heads of corporate Britain. They required people who could help them communicate with these new consumers. And they had a sense that their golf-playing, army officer chums at the agency weren't the men for the job. Suddenly, being young, bright and fashionable was a valuable commodity. David Puttnam was hired by Collett Dickenson Pearce when he was just twenty-one to work as a client liaison. 'People of my age were the only people who understood the *zeitgeist* at that time,' he says. 'The over-thirty-fives just couldn't get their heads around the pace of change or the nature of change that was taking place. So we became essential for big business. We were the conduit for established organisations to put their hands in the pockets of teenagers.'

Such was the scope of change that took place in the early sixties that it wasn't enough for companies to simply alter their marketing. Those who wanted to survive had to reassess every aspect of their business. 'I was working on the Pretty Polly account,' says Puttnam.

We were flogging their stockings with some very sexy ads but what was absolutely clear was that the girls we were selling to didn't want stockings, they wanted pantyhose. Their only interest in stockings was for Saturday night when they might go out and meet a bloke. For the rest of the week they needed practical daily wear. So I got head to head with the bosses at Pretty Polly and told them that the problem was the product. They needed to make pantyhose instead of stockings. My boss at the agency told me it wasn't our job to advise them on the products but I said, 'We've got no choice.' How could we ask them to throw their money down the drain by marketing a product that nobody wants to buy? It would cost vast amounts for them to retool their factories to change their product line but I felt that was the price they had to pay. That was the story of British industry in that era. The ones that were prepared to accept the fact that markets were changing and changed their products accordingly survived; the ones who tried to compete by making the same old products died.

The young generation of admen discovered a new zest for their jobs. Their initial ambivalence towards the work disappeared and their eyes were opened to the vast creative potential of advertising. This realisation was single-handedly inspired by exposure to the work being produced by Doyle Dane Bernbach in New York.

'DDB was the single influence on all of us,' says Alan Parker. 'Primarily it was the press ads that we started to see for Volkswagen and Avis. We adored it. Not just because of the great ideas and great writing but the beautiful, revolutionary art direction too.' Bill Bernbach's distinctive style of advertising soon became essential reference material for every young creative in the British industry. 'Almost every ad I'd seen in Britain was pretty awful,' recalls John Webster. 'Then one day a colleague showed me all this DDB stuff and said, "This is what you can do." It was brilliant work, quite brilliant. They were wonderful masterpieces.' Soon, it became the only benchmark. 'I started to win awards at Mather and Crowther but they didn't mean much to me once I'd seen the stuff coming out of DDB,' says Webster. 'I wasn't satisfied being judged against other British work. I thought we were so behind America that our whole industry needed a total shake-up.'

By 1962 there was a loose group of young admen spread across London, all of whom were linked by their love of Doyle Dane Bernbach's advertising. Each of them resolved to elevate their own work to similar standards. But each of them was frustrated by the rigid infrastructures that prevented them from doing so. Ad agency bosses were theoretically coming round to a more creative culture and were backed by clients who were keen to cash in on the bright young things of swinging London. But: 'We were still at the stage of writers slipping their words under art director's doors,' says

Alan Parker. 'There was no collaboration and the atmosphere wasn't geared around the creative process.' And while account executives were happy to pay lip-service to their young creative stars, they retained much of the real power. 'I remember pitching for the Hoover account at one agency,' says Sid Roberson.

> I did some good work and we won the business. So I went to the boss and said, 'I won us that business, I want a pay rise.' He said to me: 'Firstly, you're already as well paid as anyone else in this department. And secondly, the reason we won that business is that Jeremy in accounts plays golf with the chairman of Hoover.'

Young creatives identified the need for a shift in the balance of power. In order to genuinely improve the creative standards of their work, they felt that they – not the account men – should be the dominant forces within agencies. 'I needed to have more control over the sort of work we were producing,' says John Webster. 'But it was such an establishment on the board of Mather and Crowther that I knew it wouldn't be possible there. So in the end, the only way to get ahead really was to leave.' But there were few agencies in London where the culture was any different. Ultimately, the young creatives were forced to bide their time and attempt to change attitudes from the inside. 'Creative departments had never really seemed to take the work they did seriously,' says David Abbott. 'Our generation had to work hard to alter that impression. I, from the start, was interested in copywriting per se. I realised to be good at it you've got to do it to the exclusion of everything else. And once I'd discovered copywriting, I stopped wanting to write anything else.'

The face of creative departments had changed. Gone were introverted, pipe-smoking poets, shamefacedly churning out cheap slogans. In came an altogether more dynamic band of writers and designers. What they lacked in formal training they made up for in ambition and application. They resolved to transform their work into a credible and respected creative discipline. They aspired to match the brilliance of the advertising produced by their heroes in New York. Eventually, they hoped to better it. And along with their new creative verve came a bullish, insistent attitude. 'It was no good us producing brilliant, innovative work if our account men couldn't convince the clients to buy it,' says Sid Roberson.

> So we decided that we had to make the account men more scared of us oiks in the creative department than they were of the toffs at the client's offices. We'd terrify them. We'd give them our ideas and say, 'Go and sell this to the client and don't come back and tell us they didn't like it, you cunt!' Basically, we bullied the work through.

While the new generation of creatives tightened their grip on the fusty agencies of London, a further development was to bolster their crusade. The men responsible for much of the inspiring work coming out of New York were on their way across the Atlantic. These were men whose flair and enthusiasm matched that of their young British counterparts. Unlike their British counterparts, they wielded enough power to make genuine changes to the structure of the industry. Within two years of their arrival, British advertising would never be the same again.

3

'You're Never Alone with a Strand'

In August 1960 the SS *Liberté* sailed from New York into South-ampton carrying a cargo that would help spark the revolution in British advertising. On board was Robert Brownjohn, one of New York's hottest young graphic designers. But as he stepped off the boat, his wife and young daughter in tow, he hardly looked like a saviour. Pale, drawn and skinny, he hadn't slept for the whole journey. 'I met him off the boat-train at Paddington,' says Alan Fletcher, the London designer who would introduce Brownjohn to the local industry. 'He'd tried to go cold turkey on the way over and it had been a rough journey. He looked like shit.'

London in 1960 had little to offer the Bright Young Things of New York. Exchanging the heady excitement of Madison Avenue's creative revolution for London's advertising backwater seemed an improbable move. But not for Brownjohn, whose reputation as a brilliant designer was matched only in scale by his catastrophic heroin addiction. Having founded Brownjohn, Chermayeff and Geimer and turned it into one of New York's most innovative design companies in the fifties, he was in dire need of a break. While at BCG, he had earned a prestigious reputation thanks largely to his work on Pepsi-Cola's in-house monthly magazine, *Pepsi-Cola World*. Brownjohn designed a series of stylish covers that took a skewed look at the famous Pepsi logo. His professional life might have been buoyant but his destructive personal habits were threatening to ruin him. 'If someone says "I'm going out to get cigarettes, I'll be back in fifteen minutes," and you spend the next three days fielding telephone calls from his wife, you know there is something wrong,' said his New York business partner Ivan Chermayeff. 'You could be talking to BJ [Brownjohn], with all these other people in the room, and BJ would be out like a light on the table. He was pretty far over the edge.'

Inevitably, Brownjohn's position in the company became untenable. When he began to look for a place to start his life anew, London had one obvious appeal: the British allowed heroin to be prescribed to registered addicts. He would sail to England in a drastic attempt to drag himself back to sobriety. Finding work wouldn't turn out to be a problem. Brownjohn arrived in London at a time of immense openness to American design and advertising. His arrival was flattering to those within the creative industries who looked upon their New York counterparts with starry-eyed reverence. Brownjohn's radical ideas, fresh approach and carousing swagger embodied the broader influence that a whole set of Americans would have over the next five years.

It was not the first time American arrivals would impact upon British advertising. J Walter Thompson had first arrived on British shores in 1900. Already one of the biggest agencies in the United States, it had established itself in London as a conduit for European companies wishing to buy American media space. In 1926, it morphed into something more akin to a modern advertising agency, introducing swish new practices from the USA. The British Market Research Bureau was set up and owned by JWT in the early 1930s, becoming the first company of its kind in Britain. By 1933, JWT was one of the top three agencies in the country. After the war, other American agencies arrived in London. Not all of them were keen on stretching their already profitable operations to such a meagre, rain-soaked market. But their clients were already expanding across the Atlantic and made it quite clear: handle our marketing in Europe or don't handle it at all. And so giants of Madison Avenue such as McCann-Erickson, Foote, Cone and Belding and the Ted Bates agency soon followed JWT, somewhat reluctantly, to Britain.

They didn't find it difficult to find new business once they had arrived. Their methods were slicker, they had more experience and they offered a greater range of marketing services than their British rivals. The fact that they represented just one branch of an international network seemed impossibly glamorous and sophisticated to British clients. In post-war London, many indigenous British agencies collapsed under the strain of American competition. By the mid-1950s, US agencies were fast taking control of British advertising.

On the surface, JWT's London office was hardly American: its Berkeley Square headquarters were opulently adorned with Regency furniture and staffed by the gentlest of British businessmen. Its professional conduct owed a great deal more to village-green cricket than New York's aggressive business culture. 'It was extremely British,' says Jeremy Bullmore, who started as a copywriter at JWT in 1954. 'I think this was largely because transatlantic air travel wasn't easily available yet so people were left to get on with things.'

But however fusty the agency's outward appearance might have been, its methods were thoroughly modern. When Bullmore attended his interview for a copywriter's role aged twenty-five, little interest was shown in his creative abilities. 'I was interviewed by Norman Bassett, head of the copy department, who told me about the Great Margarine War,' he recalled. 'And by a psychologist, who asked me what I thought about a series of obscene ink blots.' This scientific approach to advertising was rapidly growing in popularity. Rationing had ended in 1955 and, for the first time since the war, supplies exceeded demand. No longer were consumers grateful to shopkeepers for providing them with products. Now, they had a wealth of genuine choices; it was a buyer's market. Those doing the selling had to work harder to gain attention for their products. 'The biggest American influence prior to the sixties was applying this almost academic approach to understanding the market,' says Bullmore. 'The question they posed was: "If we do not know what our market looks like, if we don't know who they are, if we don't know what's on their minds, how can we talk to them?"'

Still, little emphasis was put on how the advertisement might be delivered. JWT, the so-called 'University of Advertising', had successfully instilled a stern mistrust of frivolous 'creativity'. As far back as 1906, the agency had published a guide entitled *The Thompson Blue Book on Advertising* which clearly outlined their principles on the subject. 'Good advertising is the product of concentrated thought working with tested methods and full-blooded organisation for the accomplishment of profit-making results,' it stated. 'Neither haphazard inspiration nor novel theories nor meagre equipment has any place in a modern advertising campaign.'

By the time television advertising emerged in the UK in 1955, these sound American principles had rendered British advertising a thoroughly professional industry. Early commercials provided a blunt but effective impact. 'I want to advertise on TV and I want a jingle,' was the simplistic brief given by shirt manufacturer Harry Raelbrook to musician Johnny Johnston in 1957. 'What's so special about your shirts?' asked Johnston. 'You don't need to iron them,' explained Raelbrook. With that, Johnston sat down at a piano and, beginning to play, sang seven words: 'Raelbrook Toplin, the shirts you don't iron!' He repeated the slogan three times, then changed key and repeated the process. Raelbrook was thrilled: 'That's what I want! Don't change anything!'

This simplistic, battering-ram approach seemed to work. A 1955 commercial for Murray Mints featured animated guards, complete with bearskin hats, outside Buckingham Palace. 'Murray Mints, Murray Mints, too good to hurry mints!' went the jingle, which had been recorded by Cliff Adams and the Stargazers. About three months into the campaign, the band appeared on *Sunday Night at the London Palladium* and ended their set with a rendition of the jingle. They performed the number dressed in bearskins, which they removed at the climax, revealing hidden packets of Murray Mints, which were thrown into the audience. The stunt caused a minor sensation and proved that, even in television's fledgling years, oft-repeated ad slogans were embedding themselves in the public's minds.

Occasionally, attempts were made to appeal to viewers by more subtle means. In 1959, an advert for Strand cigarettes paid ambitious homage to Hollywood's film-noir genre. A handsome actor with Frank Sinatra looks was shown walking down a darkened street. To the strains of a moody, wordless soundtrack (again composed by Cliff Adams), he stopped to light a Strand. The commercial ended with a line that, relative to other slogans of the time, was positively enigmatic: 'You're never alone with a Strand'. It was a disaster. Sales of the product actually fell as a result, with the public apparently convinced that Strand was the preferred cigarette of lonely, unpopular night crawlers. Traditional advertising values were vindicated: ambiguity, nuance and economy of style were no match for confrontational imagery and explicit sloganeering.

'I'm coming to London and I am looking for any kind of work, can you help me?' wrote Robert Brownjohn to his small number of contacts in 1960. He was renowned for convention-defying design, but his experience of making advertisements was almost non-existent. As well as his famous *Pepsi-Cola World* covers, he had won acclaim for numerous paperback covers for the publisher Simon and Schuster. His style was simple and striking and his sensibilities were those of a commercial graphic designer. Nonetheless, his New York credentials were enough to convince British agencies of his value. 'BJ wrote to me, or called me, asking me to get him a job,' recalled Bob Gill, another New York designer who had arrived in London some months earlier to work at the Charles Hobson advertising agency. 'I said, "You're a great designer, you don't need me. If you can straighten yourself out, you can come here and be a big shot, because you'll be the best art director in the country."'

Brownjohn and his family moved into Campden Hill Towers, a newly built tower block on Notting Hill Gate that was developing into what Gill described as 'a beautiful vignette of London'. Gill and Alan Fletcher, the leading British designer, lived on the floor above Brownjohn along with the future television personality Bamber Gascoigne. Dudley Moore was a regular visitor to the building, which quickly became a hub of young, creative Londoners. Soon, Brownjohn found work at J Walter Thompson. 'He gave me a magazine, *Typographica* . . . in which there was some of the work he had done with Chermayeff and Geismer,' said Willie Landels, then head of JWT's art department. 'I looked at it and said, "Great, come and work for us."' Brownjohn was very quickly elevated to the level of creative director. JWT may have possessed an inherent hostility to creative mavericks like Brownjohn but finding people as talented as him in London wasn't easy. 'London in 1960 was amateurs-ville,' said Gill. 'It was like shooting fish in a barrel. We were so obviously number one, there was no question. We ended up doing everything.' Gill had been planning a holiday to Europe when he spotted an ad in the *New York Times* seeking a creative director for an English agency. He attended the interview in a Manhattan hotel with the intention of working in London for a month. 'The guy took one look at my work and said, "We'll hire you,"' he remembered. 'I said, "I only want to stay for a month" – I was on a roll in New York, I was a hot designer – but he said, "Come anyway!" I knew I was going to stay for a while as soon as I got off the plane. There was something about the chemistry, it was such an adventure, like landing on the moon.' But he remained unimpressed with British advertising. 'The guy who hired me was called Nicholas Kay, he was a fifty-five-year-old, very square Englishman with an umbrella and bowler. He was paying me more than the prime minister was making, he thought the sun shone out of my ass. But it was a hack agency and I wasn't interested.'

Brownjohn, meanwhile, was happy to exploit the reverence shown to him by his new employers at JWT. 'He would turn up late at the office and go straight out to lunch,' says Alan Fletcher, who became friends with Brownjohn.

> He liked a drink in the afternoon, often to deal with the hangover from the night before. But he got paid vast sums of money compared to the rest of us because he was so smart and entertaining. Agencies were just happy to have him around, wheel him out for clients once in a while. Like Gill and the other Americans who had come over at that time, he was exceptionally smart. They weren't has-beens who couldn't get jobs in New York, they were brilliant men on an adventure in a foreign country.

One of Brownjohn's earliest successes was on behalf of a designer at a rival agency. Willie Landels' wife, Angela, was working at Coleman Prentice and Varley on an advertisement for Yardley lipsticks when her husband brought Brownjohn home one night. 'He said, "Oh, I've got this great idea." Then he told me this marvellous idea of the gun holster with the lipstick as bullets,' she recalled. 'He gave me the headline too, "A Woman's Ammunition".' The image was striking and the premise bold. It was a simple idea underpinned by a gentle wit; in other words, it was everything that safe, formal British advertising had never been before. Landels was adamant that she couldn't use someone else's idea but Brownjohn insisted she did so, denying that he wanted any credit. 'Embarrassingly enough it won every award going,' she said. 'And Yardley's lipsticks went from fifth in the market to second, which was amazing . . . Initially Brownjohn was very pleased but the more publicity it got the more he resented it. I don't blame him.'

Adrian Lyne (who would later become a successful director of Hollywood movies, including *Fatal Attraction*) had gone to work as a messenger in the JWT mailroom in 1960. Running errands in such a vast company felt 'like working as a bellboy in a run-down hotel'. He had little interest in advertising but revelled in the cosmopolitan environment. 'There were such a lot of characters there,' he says.

> Very colourful and interesting people. Frank Lowe started around the same time as a controller. I used to take work around the building for him. Most of my friends were the Jamaican guys who worked in the mailroom with me. They would take me to these reggae clubs in the evening with them. I was introduced to a whole new exciting world. But what sickened me was that I knew those guys wouldn't get a promotion because they were black. I only had to do six months in the mailroom before I was put on a funny training scheme and sent to work in the TV department.

It was there that Lyne first encountered Brownjohn. 'He was rail thin, emaciated,' he recalls. 'I heard he'd taken a heroin cure on the boat on the way over, he'd been a junkie and was friends with Miles Davis. I loved that kind of jazz. I was infatuated with this man. He was immensely talented and would generate your enthusiasm.' It was enough to set the young messenger down a path that would eventually lead him to superstardom within the industry. 'He [Brownjohn] turned into an alcoholic and ballooned into an enormous person,' he laments. 'But he inspired an excitement in me about advertising. It was all caught up in this fabulous atmosphere that was beginning to build in Soho. There was a lot of eccentricity, a sort of madness going on.'

Brownjohn embodied a new type of adman who seemed in complete harmony with the changing mood of the industry. More and more young people saw it as the industry to work in. 'All the

Americans arriving completely influenced me,' says Hugh Hudson, who was an aspiring film director when he met Brownjohn in the early sixties. The pair would eventually form a production company together. 'He influenced me terribly: the simplicity of his way of looking at things and his directness. Somehow, he set standards for me that I lived by all my life.' Young Brits with big creative ideas were growing in number but were struggling to make their voices heard within large, old-fashioned agencies. But when similar ideas were expressed with an American accent, they carried more weight. 'The likes of Brownjohn and Bob Gill were the ones putting new creative ideas out there,' says Hudson.

> Being American carried a great deal of credibility at that time. They might have been working mainly in design but the principles they observed began to trickle down into all forms of advertising. They really were breaking new ground. They were the fountain-head for all the change that was happening.

A year after Bob Gill had arrived in London, and six months after Brownjohn, a third American named Bob hit town. His name was Bob Brooks and his influence would outweigh even that of his namesakes. Born in Philadelphia, he had graduated in finance from Pennsylvania University before joining the Quartermaster stores as a time and efficiency manager. While working in their New York offices, he began to make friends from a world very different to his own. 'I got to know people who were artists, designers and architects,' he says. 'I began to realise that I had to be involved in their world. I didn't know specifically what I wanted to do but I sensed that to be creative in New York at that moment was the right path to follow.' He enrolled at New York's Cooper Union College, one of America's most esteemed art schools. His artistic leaning having been unexpectedly awoken, he quit his job at the Quarter-master stores and took a work placement at an art studio. 'I thought that might have been the way to go,' he says. 'But then I discovered that to work in a big art studio you needed to be good at drawing. I was horrible at drawing so I looked elsewhere.' Cooper Union's employment agency found him an apprenticeship at Hewitt, Ogilvy, Benson and Mather, one of Manhattan's most esteemed advertising agencies. This suited his aspirations much more closely: Cooper Union schooled its students in the design theories of Germany's Bauhaus art school, all of which were underpinned by the idea that 'form follows function'. For Brooks, a young man with a creative mind but little technical skill, these theories were appealing. And he soon found that they could be practically applied to advertising. 'It was great as soon as I got there,' he says of the agency.

I knew that this was my business. It was around this time that illustration was dying out in press ads. In the forties and early fifties all art directors had been frustrated illustrators adorning their ads with drawings. But suddenly photography became the big thing. So as an art director all you needed to do was come up with a great idea and commission the photographer. It was your ideas that mattered, not your personal ability to deliver them.

Soon, Brooks had moved on to Benton and Bowles, where he swiftly worked his way up to the position of creative group head thanks largely to a winning idea for one of their most important clients, Crest toothpaste. His press advertisement depicted a young boy coming out of a dentist's surgery, greeting his mother with the words 'Look ma, no cavities!' The idea went on to spawn a long running TV campaign and the slogan passed into widespread use. Brooks was quickly making a name for himself in the heady atmosphere of Madison Avenue but was restless. When Benton and Bowles opened a London office, he begged them to let him go there. 'I loved the idea of living in Europe but they told me they weren't sending anybody over from New York to London,' he says.

Desperate to experience European life, Brooks eventually accepted an offer from rival agency McCann-Erickson to work in their

Milan office. 'When Benton and Bowles heard they ended up offering me a job in London after all,' he says. 'By that stage I wasn't interested. I really didn't want to go to London because I thought its advertising was no good and I loved Italy. But eventually they made me a very good offer and I said, "You win."'

Still in his twenties, Brooks arrived in London in 1961 and was installed as the head of Benton and Bowles' art department. He was unimpressed with what he found. 'I wasn't sure what I'd walked into,' he says. 'The first two years in London were not what I would call exciting. It was just a constant battle within the agency to get some decent work through. I even went to see creative heads at other big agencies but their work was generally ordinary and really quite boring. It was such a contrast to what was going on in New York.' The fiery-tempered art director found the atmosphere almost intolerable.

> It was a fight within my agency to breathe in fresh air. It could often get quite physical and violent. I already had a reputation from New York when I arrived in London. I would shout and throw people out of the office. I remember one junior account man who I instructed to sell an idea to a tricky client. I told him, 'You've got to sell this ad, nothing else will work!' But the asshole didn't do it! He went to see the client and faltered! He came into my office to tell me and I could feel disaster looming within myself. I don't know what possessed me but I grabbed him by his tie and shoved him against the wall and smashed a big glass-framed painting, screaming at the top of my lungs. I managed to pull him back at the last second before one of the shards went straight through him. The whole creative department came rushing in to see what had happened.

Brooks displayed a passion that provided both inspiration and fear among his colleagues. His tantrums would eventually form the template for self-styled creative 'mavericks' who sought to gain attention within the industry. But for Brooks, the fiery outbursts had a serious purpose. 'I knew I had to fight to change the way people thought about advertising here [in London],' he says. 'For me it was a point of pride that we did the work properly, to a very high standard. If we Americans brought anything over to London at that time it was what we saw as a sense of professionalism.'

Brooks resolved that he should use his fast-growing profile within the British industry to help change it. 'There were several things that really annoyed me about the British industry when I first got there,' he says. 'I thought that art directors were considered the inferior part of the creative team. I hated the way they were referred to as "visualisers". One of the first things I did at Benton and Bowles was change their titles. The other big problem I saw was the Layton Awards.' Layton was a London printing and block-making company that worked for most of the leading advertising agencies. There was an unwritten agreement between Layton and the agencies that allowed entries to be submitted as 'designed or created on a group basis'. 'For creative directors and agencies the system was great. But it meant that creatives were often uncredited for their ideas and that was a terrible hindrance to their careers. That upset me,' says Brooks. 'It was a system that meant that many of the best creatives in town remained unknown and couldn't get better jobs or bigger salaries. I wanted to change it.'

Brooks was already a member of the New York Art Directors Club, which held a prestigious annual show that had instilled the US industry with a healthy competitiveness. Brooks resolved to establish a similar group in London and sought out like-minded individuals to assist him. 'I had an immediate rapport with Colin Millward, who had just started as creative director at Collett Dickenson Pearce,' remembers Brooks. 'I called him and he said, "You must come with me to the headquarters." This turned out to be La Terraza, a fantastic Italian restaurant in Soho. It was incredible: every mover and shaker in the industry was there, crammed into his corny little room.' There, amidst a gaggle of fellow ad executives who were oblivious to their scheming, Brooks and Millward met with Malcolm Hart, an art director from the ad agency Bensons, and Bob Greers, whom Brooks had recently recruited from New York. They decided that they would set up a London Art Directors' Club with the prime purpose of staging an annual advertising awards competition for both print and television. Membership in the club would be limited to those persons whose work was accepted in the annual show and the 'group basis' crediting system would be abolished. 'Names would be named!' says Brooks.

Brooks was contacted by Alan Fletcher, who explained that he and a group of London graphic designers were planning to form a similar organisation within their industry. The two groups met and eventually decided that they should combine their efforts and form the Designers and Art Directors Association, or D&AD. John Commander, an art director at the printing firm Balding and Mansell, was elected chairman. 'Our immediate task was to stage the first annual D&AD competition,' recalls Brooks. 'A stellar jury was selected consisting of some of the best names in London design and advertising. We even created an electronic voting system to keep the process as unbiased and secret as possible.' Colin Forbes, a leading graphic designer, devised a suitably simplistic logo for the association and, in 1966, Lou Klein would design a trophy that would fast become the industry's defining icon. The fat yellow pencils that were awarded at each year's D&AD ceremony became the industry's most coveted prize.

In 1962, D&AD staged its first awards ceremony at the London Hilton with Lord Snowdon opening the exhibition. 'The Layton Awards scheme was finished,' says Brooks. 'And D&AD was on its way.' From that day onwards, advertising changed for ever. Writers and designers had exposure and incentive. Ambition and competitiveness reigned. It instilled a sense of celebrity in the industry whereby award winners would be pointed at and spoken of in hushed tones over the tables at La Terrazza. Agencies began to covet their rivals' top creative performers and salaries began to spiral as a poaching culture set in. Often, a single appearance in D&AD's yearly showcase annual (referred to with solemn reverence throughout the industry as 'the book') was enough to earn the advertisement's creators a big-money transfer to a new agency. In the decades that followed, the industry and its clients became dangerously preoccupied by the acquisition of those yellow pencils. As Jeremy Bullmore observes:

> D&AD probably did more good than harm but it certainly did a great deal of harm. It instilled a false sense of value in a particular kind of creative work that wasn't necessarily the best type of work commercially. It allowed many advertising people to convince themselves that they were fine artists as opposed to people working in a commercial business.

Such were the high standards set by the judges that the prestigious 'Gold Award' wasn't given out every year but reserved for occasional works of particular brilliance. An early recipient of such an award was Robert Brownjohn for his title sequence to the 1964 James Bond film *Goldfinger*. It set a template for the genre, featuring a beautiful, silhouetted girl dancing while the credits shimmered across her body. Alan Fletcher recalls how Brownjohn initially presented the idea to Bond producer Cubby Broccoli.

> He turned up for the meeting at a screening theatre in Wardour Street. The producers were all looking for his portfolio but all he had with him was a pocket full of thirty-five-millimetre slides. They asked him how he proposed to do their title sequence, at which point he put the slides in the carousel, switched it on, took off his shirt and started dancing in front of it. Luckily, Broccoli seemed able to interpret what he was trying to say.

4

'The Man in the Hathaway Shirt'

There were three distinct types of American advertising agency in the mid-sixties and their contrasting cultures were neatly encapsulated by the manner in which their receptionists answered the telephone. At Ogilvy and Mather, the grand agency established by legendary Brit David Ogilvy, callers would be received with a polite 'Ogilvy and Mather, how can I help you?' At BBDO, a smaller mainstream agency that aspired to respectability, the phone was answered with an almost sycophantic: 'BBDO, what is your pleasure?' But at Papert, Koenig and Lois, a swaggering young agency at the forefront of the creative revolution, the greeting was rather more forthright: 'This is PKL,' barked the receptionist. 'Who the fuck are you?'

In 1963 London's adland braced itself for the arrival of PKL. They were the quintessential New York 'hot shop': an agency formed by Doyle Dane Bernbach alumni who'd already taken New York awards ceremonies by storm and were intent on showing Europe how it was done. They waltzed into London with the same arrogant swagger that US servicemen had carried on to British shores during the Second World War. This American agency was hip, smart and sneering – and the British ad industry loved it.

British advertising had made steady progress since the establishment of D&AD. Creativity had acquired a new value, clients were supportive of the agencies' new style of working and the young admen who had previously felt frustrated by the industry were finally making their voices heard. But it wasn't until the first of America's hot young agencies arrived that London would acquire some of Madison Avenue's glamorous, exciting and slightly dangerous frisson.

In December 1963, PKL's first Christmas party was the talk of London's advertising scene. The agency had resided in its poky Sloane Street offices for less than a year but had already established a reputation for producing innovative work. Its staff of unkempt creatives were known just as well for their hell-raising antics as they were for their professional endeavours. By the mid-sixties, tales of drinking, fighting and womanising within advertising were nothing new. Every agency had its maverick wild man by then: whether it was Robert Brownjohn lying unconscious on heroin at JWT or Bob Brooks attacking account executives at Benton and Bowles. What was different about PKL was that gross misbehaviour was not the exception but the rule. Visitors to that year's Christmas party approached the Sloane Square venue with a mixture of excitement and trepidation. None of them was prepared for what they found when they walked through the doors. Blood splattered the desks, walls and carpets of the boardroom. All around, some of the industry's brightest young stars desperately mopped and scrubbed at the horrific mess, wearing pale-faced expressions of astonishment. It was perhaps inevitable that PKL's first Christmas party would feature mass bloodshed.

The blood was that of agency chairman Nigel Sealey. His assailant was Tony Palladino, the American art director who had been dispatched by the New York office to set up their London operation. He had quickly helped establish a band of would-be British admen who were desperate to learn the secrets of American advertising. The young recruits generated a heady atmosphere of intense competitiveness and rampant hedonism. At the Christmas party, tensions spilled over quickly. 'Tony decided he was going to thump Nigel,' remembers Peter Mayle.

> Before anyone could stop him he'd made a lunge at Nigel, who was holding a glass of wine. Instinctively, he raised his hand to shield his face but Tony's fist rammed the glass into his throat. It got him right in the jugular and blood started spurting out everywhere. We managed to stem the bleeding and get him off to Accident and Emergency where, somehow, they managed to save his life. Meanwhile, the rest of us were left to scrub the entire boardroom of his blood.

As he surveyed the chaos, Peter Mayle (who years later would find great success as the writer of books such as *A Year in Provence*) briefly contemplated why he'd ever returned to London. Three years previously, he had given up on Britain and moved to America to pursue his dream of writing advertisements. 'London advertising was medieval in those days,' he says. 'The ads were terrible and I couldn't get a job anywhere. I hadn't been to university and studied poetry, which is what agencies seemed to want back then.'

The ambitious young Mayle heard about the changes that were taking place in the American industry and supposed that New York's egalitarian climate would allow him greater opportunities. 'I'd read about David Ogilvy and decided that he was the man to contact,' he says. Mayle was setting his sights about as high as they could go. Ogilvy was a British expat who had casually taken the American ad industry by storm. As he bluntly surmised in a memoir: 'I had gone to New York and started an advertising agency. Americans thought I was crazy. What could a Scotsman know about advertising? My agency was an *immediate* and *meteoric* success.'

Ogilvy swept into the advertising industry at the relatively late age of thirty-eight. Having previously worked as an oven salesman in Scotland (a job at which he excelled) and a trainee chef in Paris, he eventually arrived in New York and worked for several years at the pioneering market research firm, Gallup. After a brief spell spent farming tobacco, he took a job as a copywriter and swiftly opened his own agency with the backing of London's Mather and Crowther. He started with just $6,000 in his account, no clients and less than ten staff, but had soon attracted blue-chip accounts such as American Express, Schweppes and Rolls-Royce. He based a great deal of emphasis on research techniques and utilised all that he had learnt at Gallup. He used the research to establish creative rules that would maximise the impact of his advertisements in every detail. 'In one year at Ogilvy as a junior creative I learned more about advertising theory than I did for the next twenty years,' says Bob Brooks. 'Ogilvy had used his research methods to work out which typefaces worked best, where headlines should be placed, the exact size in which pictures should appear, why photography was better than illustration. All of these things became steadfast rules of the industry.'

Ogilvy fused this scientific approach with an enthusiasm for elegant creative work. He became renowned for the literary style of his press advertisements and made his name with a flurry of iconic campaigns. He devised 'The Man in the Hathaway Shirt', featuring a dapper-looking aristocrat in an incongruous eyepatch. Hathaway was a shirt manufacturer from Maine with an unfashionable image. Ogilvy conjured the idea of a sophisticated oddball to serve as the face of the company. The first press ads appeared in 1951 and featured a photograph of the lean, moustachioed figure wearing an almost disdainful expression. The text outlined the high quality of his shirts. But soon, the image became so iconic that the ads ran without mention of the Hathaway brand name. In fact, the gentleman's signature item became his eyepatch rather than his shirts.

Nonetheless, Hathaway's sales tripled within two years. Ogilvy's campaign was heralded by the advertising industry as a creative breakthrough. He had proved that ads didn't have to talk explicitly about the product. All consumers knew about Hathaway shirts was that they were worn by a cool-looking man with one eye. That seemed to be enough.

Ogilvy repeated the technique for Schweppes. 'The Man from Schweppes Is Here' campaign introduced American consumers to Commander Whitehead, a genuine Schweppes executive who was successfully transformed into the face of the company. Perhaps Ogilvy's most famous headline was for Rolls-Royce: 'At sixty miles an hour, the loudest noise in this new Rolls-Royce comes from the electric clock.'

His agency went from strength to strength. Rather than lobby potential clients for business, he allowed each of his campaigns to serve as public advertisements for his agency's skill. It was a successful strategy: business flew through Ogilvy's doors and he was soon presiding over one of Madison Avenue's greatest ever success stories. His advertising was talked about. He introduced the idea of brand image to the advertising world. In 1955 he told the American Association of Advertising Agencies: 'Every advertisement should be thought of as a contribution to the complex symbol which is the brand image.' These were unprecedented ideas in the fifties but soon became the foundation of every major company's marketing strategy.

Combining rigorous, research-based techniques with an intelligent brand of creativity, Ogilvy served as a bridge between New York's grand old agencies and Bill Bernbach's new advertising methods. Like many young admen, Peter Mayle was in awe of the pipe-smoking marketing guru and lobbied him incessantly for work via a series of transatlantic letters. Eventually, he got his wish and was invited over to work as a junior copywriter. Ogilvy's agency was a sprawling operation with the guru-like Scotsman at its helm. His precise teachings, right down to the preferred positioning of coupons on press advertisements, were drummed into every creative in the agency. It was the perfect training ground for someone like Mayle, who had arrived with no experience whatsoever. But after two years in the job, he began to tire of Ogilvy's rigid creative formulas. When he was offered the chance to work for an agency that purposefully flouted such processes, he was intrigued. 'Papert Koenig and Lois had only just been set up and I was particularly interested in working for George Lois,' recalls Mayle. Lois had been one of Doyle Dane Bernbach's star creatives before breaking away to establish his own agency. He was a Madison Avenue legend with a fiery personality that matched his creative reputation. As one Brit who spent the early sixties working in New York recalls: 'A colleague came back from lunch one day and said: "I've just seen the most extraordinary thing. George Lois just punched a cab out in the street!" I said, "Do you mean George Lois just punched a cab driver?" But he said, "No, he actually punched the cab!"' It was by no means the first time the art director had found himself embroiled in fisticuffs. 'George Lois was involved in a small brawl with a friend of mine, Bill Casey,' wrote Jerry Della Femina in his 1970 book on New York's ad scene, *From Those Wonderful Folks Who Brought You Pearl Harbor*.

Casey had been working at PKL and he was leaving. There was some kind of stock dispute about his leaving and so they scheduled a reconciliation meeting. Casey was the kind of guy who might have a couple of drinks in a bar and all of a sudden a brawl seems to erupt around him. Something went wrong at the reconciliation meeting and the first thing you know Lois vaults over a table and tries to take a punch at Casey. Secretaries were yelling, the usual chaos. It wasn't the greatest example of a guy leaving an agency.

According to Della Femina, Lois's antics were emulated by many of his employees. 'Back in 1965 there was a terrific fight at PKL during which an account supervisor named Bert Sugar slugged another guy, leaving blood all over the place,' he writes. 'They used to call PKL "Stillman's East", after the old fight gym.'

An agency under Lois's stewardship represented quite a contrast to one governed by Ogilvy, and PKL immediately lived up to Peter Mayle's expectations. 'It was my first experience of working directly with an art director,' he says. 'I was used to sitting in a room alone working on my copy. Suddenly, I had to go and sit with an Italian guy who would scratch his balls with one hand while designing a layout with the other. It was very stimulating.' PKL might have seemed chaotic to the outside world but, for those who worked there, the regime was intense. 'Lois would lock us all in a room and say, "You're going to find me a fucking idea!"' says Mayle. 'He would always tell us: "Don't put anything down on the page unless you're sure people will shit themselves when they see it!"'

Peter Mayle was not the only Brit to head for New York in the sixties. For numerous aspiring British admen, Madison Avenue was Mecca. Unable or unwilling to break into British advertising, they crossed the Atlantic in the hope of penetrating the industry right at its heart. But not all of them would enjoy the same success as Mayle. 'Instead of going to Thailand like they do nowadays, young creative people would head for America,' says Sid Roberson. 'After a couple of years of getting fired by various London agencies I thought I'd give it a go.' Roberson had been working at the London branch of the Ted Bates agency, who gave him a letter of introduction to their New York office. 'They had this huge building on Madison Avenue,' he says.

I had a meeting with the creative director, who had this spectacular corner office overlooking the whole of Manhattan. I'd never seen anything like it before. He told me that there was no job for me in the agency but then he said, 'Will you smile for me?' I said, 'I beg your pardon?' He asked me if I had good teeth and I told him that I did. Then he asked me if I was interested in appearing in a

48

commercial they were making. I said, 'Look, I'm an art director, not a bloody model.' And I told him to stuff it. I was a bloody jerk really because there would have been so much money in it!

Ultimately, Roberson's search for advertising work proved fruitless and he was reduced to working in a factory. 'I might not have got the job I wanted but it was a great experience anyway,' he says.

New York at that time was an inspirational place to be. I decided to educate myself because I was desperate to penetrate that kind of sophisticated, arty world. I read about everything from art to psychology to religion. I went to all the jazz clubs, hung out with Allen Ginsberg, grew a beard and started wearing a beret.

Others were more successful. After two an a half years working in junior positions at J Walter Thompson, Frank Lowe had grown restless. He was a young man in a hurry but soon discovered that his employers were unable to accommodate his ambition. 'I went to see the head of personnel and told her I wanted to be an account executive,' he says. 'She told me that I would have to wait until I was at least thirty before they would consider me. So I thought, Sod this, I'll go to America and see if I have any better luck out there.' Lowe saved enough money to fly to New York where, like Peter Mayle, he immediately identified Ogilvy and Mather as his preferred employers. 'Because of David Ogilvy, they were becoming known for hiring British people,' he says. 'But when I managed to eventually get a meeting with their chairman he told me that he couldn't hire me because they'd already taken on too many Brits.' Lowe was determined to stay in New York until he could break into advertising. To make ends meet, he took a job as a carpet salesman on Fifth Avenue. 'I found it quite easy,' he says. 'Being English was a great help because people found the accent charming and trustworthy. People would walk past the shop and I would say, "Good morning, madam, how are you today? I've got a lovely carpet for you."'

Already, the young Frank Lowe was demonstrating a knack for charm-fuelled salesmanship. Soon, he had used his powers of persuasion to find the sort of job he wanted. 'My contact at Ogilvy said he could get me in at the agency across the road from them, Benton and Bowles,' he says. 'I got a job as an account executive and loved it right away. I was still at the stage where I found advertising little more than an exciting atmosphere to work in. People seemed to come in, do a bit of work and then have lunch. It was great.' Lowe might have remained entrenched in his New York adventure for ever had war not intervened. After two years in the country, he was obliged to register for conscription to the US Army. 'I registered and was categorised as an A1 candidate which meant that I would be the first to be called up should they require extra soldiers,' he recalls. 'I thought nothing of it until the Vietnam issue began to get coverage in the press. War was looming and a friend said to me, "You know if they serve you papers and you don't join up, you'll be a draft dodger. So get out now!"' In the early sixties, there were few prospects Lowe found more grim than returning to London. But fighting in the Vietnam War was one of them, so he went home.

Dave Trott had arrived in New York with a more focused strategy than Lowe or Roberson. Having earned a scholarship to the Pratt Institute in Brooklyn, he studiously learned the principles of commercial art in a bid to infiltrate the advertising industry. 'When I got over there I saw advertising like I'd never seen before and I thought, it has to be this,' he says. 'During that period in New York, it got to the point where you felt like a schmuck if you weren't working in advertising.' Trott visited a New York exhibition showcasing the best of British advertising. 'It was cringingly embarrassing,' he says.

It looked so parochial, so small time, so weedy. It looked like Americana advertising from the fifties whereas New York was on the crest of this Bernbach revolution. There was great work all around us and then I had to stand there with my fellow students looking at this twitty exhibition of meaningless puns from my home country. So you'd have a picture of a Ford race car with the headline 'The Roaring Fordies'.

When he eventually found work in a New York advertising agency, Trott discovered the cultural advantages they held over their British counterparts. 'Americans don't have the same qualms about selling that Brits do,' he says.

> They taught me to approach an ad in the mindset of a salesman and do whatever it takes. Sometimes a joke would work best or sometimes a song or something shocking. It depended on the product. They worked their way through the problem. But Brits found selling things embarrassing and vulgar and tried to use humour as a means of distraction.

He also discovered a distinctively focused work culture. 'There was never that feudal atmosphere that existed in Britain whereby the boss was someone cracking a whip over you, making you work,' he says. 'Everyone in America wanted to work hard out of a sense of competitiveness. If a British worker saw his boss drive past in a Rolls-Royce he'd say, "What a wanker, he doesn't deserve it." Whereas an American worker would just say, "One day I'm going to have a car like that."' Ultimately, Trott's British sensibilities conflicted with this studious atmosphere. 'I was fired from one agency because I used to regularly go to the pub in my lunch hour and drink a couple of pints,' he says.

> It was natural to me because it's what I'd done when I worked in a factory back in England. But in New York I'd go back to the office and someone would say, 'Oh yeah, I knew a guy like you who had a drink problem. Used to keep a fifth of Scotch in his filing cabinet!' And they fired me. When I ended up working back in England I used to roll in drunk and stoned every afternoon. That

was the only thing that was better about the British advertising industry at the time: it tolerated eccentricity.

When Papert Koenig and Lois decided to expand into Europe, they sent creative chiefs Tony Palladino and Ron Holland to set up a London office. Peter Mayle followed them and found an agency being built in the image of its New York headquarters. 'It was a small, informal place,' he says. 'The work was considered very fresh and different for Britain at that time. And the atmosphere was the same. It was "New Yorkish" and that helped our reputation grow.' In the early sixties, British youth culture was still struggling to find an identity of its own amid the post-war gloom; young people were dependent on imported music, films and fashions from the United States. American advertising carried a similar cachet.

Finally, there was an agency that the new breed of young London admen could aspire to work at. 'As soon as they opened up here, we all applied for jobs at PKL,' says Alan Parker, who, by 1963, had worked his way up from the post room to the position of junior copywriter at Maxwell Clark. 'We'd all heard of George Lois because he was an icon of creative advertising. I went to see Peter Mayle and showed him all of the ads I'd had rejected at Maxwell Clark and he liked them.' Mayle was quick to offer Parker a job. 'I asked him how much he wanted and he said, "About fifteen." Which I thought was very reasonable,' says Mayle. Parker takes up the story: 'I got a letter a few days after the interview from Peter offering me the job on a salary of fifteen thousand pounds a year. I couldn't believe my eyes! I'd only meant fifteen pounds a week. Suddenly my salary had gone up by about one thousand per cent by mistake!'

Parker was young, scruffy and inexperienced. He was by no means a star appointment. But he was an ideal recruit for PKL, which sought to discover raw talent with an authentic touch. 'People like Parker were perfect for us because they were on the same wavelength as the people they were selling to,' says Mayle. 'They hadn't picked up all the bad middle-class habits. Give a product to an Oxbridge literary graduate and he'll go and write a bloody sonnet! The young people we hired could write ads in the sort of colloquial style that had already taken off in America.'

For their first year in London, PKL were the talk of the industry. 'People from other agencies would head over to our offices every night at six just to drink with us,' says Mayle. 'There was always a drama. One of our writers was having an affair with a photographer's girlfriend. One day the photographer found out, stormed into our offices and laid him out.' The unfortunate writer remembers the incident as a pivotal moment in his career. 'The photographer never got hired much after that but my reputation shot through the roof!' Mayle grew fond of the excitable atmosphere. 'The people we hired attracted that sort of incident. We found that difficult people always produced the best work. So our offices were filled with drinkers, fornicators and wild men. The eccentricity was great and it was a very forgiving atmosphere.'

Advertising had become a fashionable industry and PKL was the most fashionable agency at which to work. 'It had a street-smart atmosphere about it,' says Mayle. 'We had a lot of anti-establishment guys who wanted to cut the throats of all capitalists. Until they bought their first Yves Saint Laurent suits, that is. After that, they never looked back!' In mid-sixties Britain, radically left-wing politics were just as integral to a young hipster's image as wearing kaftans. With Westminster politics defined by an insipid centrist consensus, young people veered dramatically to the left. The alarming acceleration of free market capitalism prompted numerous young hippies to adopt a 'turn on, tune in, drop out' policy. They ditched work, wealth and conventional lifestyles in protest against an increasingly greedy society. Meanwhile, the self-proclaimed hippies of PKL saw no conflict between their careers and their principles. 'We'd all passionately discuss how wrong profit and greed were,' laments one former writer.

But at the same time we'd be producing ads for huge multinational companies. We weren't real hippies, we were just posturing. I used to drive around Primrose Hill delivering the *Workers Press* in my sports car! When the Workers Revolutionary Party tried to recruit me, I turned up at Vanessa Redgrave's house for the meeting in my Porsche and no one batted an eyelid!

While their young creatives were distracted by such extra-curricular pursuits, PKL's honeymoon period came to an end. In the aftermath of his ill-fated scuffle at the Christmas party, Tony Palladino decided it was time to return to New York. Ron Holland went with him, leaving a gap at the helm of the agency. The New York office took the opportunity to install a new regime in London. They were tired of hearing wild tales of bloodshed and boozing among the Brits and sent over new management from the USA with a conservative agenda. PKL moved into smart new offices in Knightsbridge and began to pursue what Mayle calls 'Big, tedious accounts like Procter & Gamble and Lever Brothers.' Esoteric creativity was discouraged in favour of a more formal approach. New York weren't interested in owning a European company with a cool reputation; they wanted respectability, growth and profit. Many of the original staffers were unimpressed. 'Suddenly, we were all confused,' says Alan Parker. 'We would attend these huge creative meetings and end up looking at each other thinking, this is absolutely not what we signed up for!' Papert Koenig and Lois had lost its nerve at the crucial moment. Staff feared that it was fast transforming into just another big, bland agency. 'The problem with the new management was that they had no PKL or Doyle Dane Bernbach pedigree,' says Parker. 'They absolutely believed in a really rather vulgar form of selling. It got to the point where they was rejecting almost every piece of work I was writing. But the more they hated it, the more I realised I was on the right track.'

Parker was the first in a flurry of creatives to quit PKL in response to the new regime. But it wasn't long before the new management proved the architects of their own demise. 'They had hired too many people and the agency was overinflated,' says Mayle. 'We didn't have enough business to support the structure they'd installed so we ended up in trouble.' The management in New York considered closing the London office. Eventually, they scaled down the business and asked Peter Mayle to take over as creative director. 'I decided to give it a go,' he says. 'It was exciting to have been elevated so quickly. I was only twenty-six, I was earning twice what the prime minister got paid and owned a house on Sloane Square.' But the seniority came at a price: Mayle's first job as creative director was to fire thirty members of staff. 'It was quite a big deal for someone my age,' he reflects. He managed to retain some of the better creative figures and tried to re-establish their reputation as a small but creatively accomplished agency. Soon they had acquired prestige clients such as Sony and Olivetti. They also gained the business of their Knightsbridge neighbours, Harrods, for whom they demon-strated their flair for simplistic, witty and counter-intuitive advertising. When the department store wanted to promote the fact that they had begun to open on Saturdays, PKL devised a commercial that would defy Harrods' grandiose image. In it, two tramps sat side by side on a bench in Hyde Park. One turned to the other and said, ' 'Ere, I see 'Arrods is open on Saturday.' The other responded with an indifferent 'Yeah', and the commercial drew to a close. Television viewers used to hard-sell, bells-and-whistles advertising had rarely seen a com-mercial that was so simplistic and confident. PKL had survived their traumatic early years and had helped change people's expectations of British advertising. But ultimately their impact would be merely symbolic. Their fleeting success proved that small, creative agencies could thrive in Britain but, as one former employee puts it: 'Our reputation was bigger than the actual business we did.' PKL marked the beginning of a British obsession with supposedly 'cool' advertis-ing. What they failed to produce was any advertising that could transcend the attentions of the industry and establish a place in the popular consciousness. Soon, an agency would emerge that spe-cialised in such work.

5

'Happiness is a Cigar Called Hamlet'

In 1962, one of Doyle Dane Bernbach's chief clients, Chemstrad, decided to launch its range of acrylic fashions in Britain and insisted that DDB follow them overseas. The American agency was reluctant to expand – but even more reluctant to lose a major account. They sought a compromise solution by approaching a small London agency called Collett Dickenson Pearce. They seemed the perfect target for a DDB takeover: they were only two years old and were trying to service a fairly substantial debt of £80,000. More pertinently, their founder, John Pearce, shared many of Bill Bernbach's core business principles. Like the American guru, he subscribed to the idea that an advertisement worked only if it was noticed, digested and remembered. Despite this, DDB weren't ready to put their agency's stellar reputation in the hands of a group of Brits. Bill Bernbach and Ned Doyle travelled to London with a clear strategy in mind: they would buy CDP, hand them the Chemstrad account but retain a tight creative control from afar. Every piece of work produced by the London office would have to be signed off by the bosses in New York.

How could this small, debt-ridden London agency resist the proposal of New York's most famous admen? John Pearce and his partner, Ronnie Dickenson, thought long and hard. Should they solve all their financial headaches by selling out and relinquishing control? Or try to work their way out of debt and then sell for a higher price? While they were trying to decide, Ned Doyle confronted John's wife, Mary Pearce, and asked her directly: 'Could your husband take orders from New York?' Whatever she said was enough to make Doyle and Bernbach break off negotiations.

Mary Pearce's response had changed the future of British advertising. DDB's influence over the industry was, by 1962, already assured. But they would regret their hesitation to enter the UK market. Within ten years, Britain would usurp America as the epicentre of the advertising industry. And central to that success would be the tiny agency they had refused to do business with: Collett Dickenson Pearce. Once they'd worked their way out of trouble, CDP went on to write the rulebook for British advertising. Over the next few decades, they would produce the most famous ads – and house the most eccentric, prolific and successful admen – the industry has ever seen.

Collett Dickenson Pearce was opened on April Fool's Day, 1960. It had been the brainchild of John Pearce and Ronnie Dickenson, who had met while working in the publishing industry. John Pearce had served in the Second World War in the South Wales Borderers. He went on to serve in the War Office, attaining the rank of lieutenant colonel, and was eventually awarded the MBE. Later, he found success as general manager of Hulton Press, overseeing popular titles such as the *Picture Press* and the *Eagle*. He was in his fifties by the time he joined the advertising industry, where he became joint managing director of Coleman Prentice and Varley, a grand and well-respected British agency. Ronnie Dickenson had served in the Royal Artillery during the war, then, like Pearce, worked for Hulton Press. Later he became a programme controller at the television company ATV. The pair's eclectic experiences in the media would inform their unusual approach to the advertising industry.

Mary Pearce remembers Ronnie Dickenson first proposing the idea of an agency to her husband. 'He dropped in for a drink at our flat in Devonshire Place one evening and said, "Why don't we start an advertising agency?"' she remembered. 'John thought it would be more interesting than the job he was doing at Coleman Prentice and Varley, so they did.'

They approached a tiny, struggling agency called Pictorial Publicity, which was owned by John Collett. It had just one client but was registered with the Institute of Practitioners in Advertising. Effectively, they had bought a ready-made agency. Dickenson was the marginally more organised of the pair and took responsibility for financial matters. John Pearce took care of client relationships and dictated the company 'philosophy': that its creative work should be the best in the business.

Pearce decided to put the creative department at the very centre of his agency. He hired Colin Millward from Coleman Prentice and Varley as creative director. Millward was a dour Yorkshireman who had been trained as an artist at Leeds College of Art and the Ecole des Beaux-Arts in Paris. Pearce granted him limitless powers to attain creative excellence. He could hire whomever he wanted. High wages would be tolerated, as would excessive behaviour – as long as the work was the best it could possibly be. Millward had a commitment to talent: he spent several hours per week looking at the work of young people; photographers, typographers, artists and writers were all subjected to his unique brand of criticism. One former creative remembers Millward responding to a layout with the question: 'Does it have to be quite so repulsive?' David Puttnam was a young account executive at the time. 'I'd walk into Colin's office with a piece of work and prop it up for him to look at,' he says. 'He'd sit there for a while nibbling his nails, then he'd mutter in his Yorkshire accent: "It's not very good, is it?" To which I'd reply, "Isn't it?" And he'd say: "No, not very good at all." I'd ask, "What don't you like about it?" And all he'd say was: "You work it out, son. Take it away. Do it again. Come back tomorrow."' The young Alan Parker remembers receiving similar feedback. 'He would stare at a piece of work and then, without looking at you, ask, "Trying to make a name for yourself, are you, son?" Then he'd just walk away.' Nonetheless, Millward became a mentor to Parker. 'He might have been blunt but he was the single most important person in advertising's so-called creative revolution,' he says.

CDP's early successes were achieved in press advertising. John Pearce used his knowledge of publishing to maximise the impact their ads would have on the public. He obsessed over matching the right advertisements to the right publications. This was an unusual approach at the time; most agencies would simply purchase the lowest-priced ad space they could find. 'In my view, John Pearce had an understanding of the media that was unique in advertising at that time,' said Brian Nicholson, the then advertising manager of the *Sunday Times*.

In 1961, Nicholson had launched the *Sunday Times* colour supplement, which Pearce immediately identified as the perfect fit for many of CDP's clients. CDP's work for Benson and Hedges, Aer Lingus, Whitbread, Chemstrad and Harvey's Bristol Cream quickly made the magazine a showcase for the most stylish photographers in Britain. Millward had spared no expense in the pursuit of aesthetic perfection: Terence Donovan, David Bailey, Helmut Newton and David Montgomery were hired to photograph the advertisements. The supplement's editor, Mark Boxer, commented, 'The sense of style and the creativity of the ads from CDP have set us at the *Sunday Times* standards to match in the editorial.' Soon, other agencies were clamouring to place their ads in the magazine. The *Observer* and the *Sunday Telegraph* launched their own rival supplements and a lucrative new medium was established.

'John Pearce encouraged us to present ads in ways that hadn't been done before,' says David Puttnam. 'We were hired by Self-ridges and I convinced the client to run whole page advertisements in the *Evening Standard* every day of the week. It hadn't been done before and the ad manager was appalled by the excess of it. He thought the whole world had gone mad. But it was a success.' The giant ads, devised by the young pairing of Charles Saatchi and Ross Cramer, emphasised the eclectic nature of the department store. Each of them stressed the appeals of a different department: from the bespoke cake-baking service ('When your kid passes his exams, say it with flour,' read the headline) to ladies' fashions ('It takes more than chic to wear this suit. It takes 44" hips'). The design featured black-and-white imagery and bold typography on stark white backgrounds – a clear assumption of the Doyle Dane Bernbach style. Presented in such an unusually large format, they were a revelation.

While Millward upped the creative standards, Pearce was re-inventing the way in which ads were consumed by the public. 'Instead of having ten small ads, John Pearce would always say, "Let's just have one massive one,"' says Alan Parker.

> I think it was a reaction to the whole dour 1950s thing. We had a brave, anarchic attitude and were unafraid about trying new stuff. We got a real mischievous pleasure out of opening a newspaper which would be deadly dull and seeing your huge advertisement stuck in the middle looking much more interesting than anything else inside.

Such extravagance depended on sympathetic clients. 'We sought out companies who had the same attitudes as us,' says Puttnam.

> Those who trusted our instincts were rewarded with successful campaigns. But those who interfered were usually given the short shrift. Alan Parker produced a series of great ads for Ford but they incessantly tried to change them. In the end John Pearce sacked

them as a client! They were easily the biggest client we had at the time. But Pearce had the guts to do it and, within a few months, we'd found another car client to replace them.

Such behaviour astonished the rest of the advertising community. 'I was with John Pearce one Christmas when I bumped into my old boss from another agency,' remembers Puttnam.

He said to us, 'The trouble with you CDP people is that you don't understand the rules!' We took this as a good thing. But the rest of the advertising industry seemed to hate John because he was disturbing the cosy relationship that had existed between agencies and clients for many years.

Colin Millward had a similarly fresh approach to client relations. Most agencies would present a number of creative options to clients and allow them to choose their favourite. But Millward established a rule whereby CDP offered just one idea. 'It was a case of take it or leave it,' says Frank Lowe, who would eventually replace Puttnam as an account executive. 'You were given one piece of work and sent to convince the clients to buy it. If you succeeded, your bosses liked you. If you failed, they didn't. That was the simple rule I learned about how to succeed at CDP.'

Lowe got to grips with Colin Millward's methods at an early stage. During his first month, he witnessed a fellow account executive walk into the creative director's office clutching an advertisement for Harvey's Bristol Cream. Nervously, he told Millward that he'd just returned from Harvey's head office in Bristol with some feedback on the work. Without looking up, Millward asked him to talk him through their responses.

'They like the ad in principle,' beamed the account man. 'But there were just a couple of problems. There were a few worries about the photograph and they thought the headline wasn't as direct as it could be. And in the body copy, just a few changes that I've agreed

61

with them there.' With that, Millward turned away and began discussing a separate matter with his secretary. Eventually, the account executive interrupted. 'Well, Colin, what should I do?' Millward turned back to him, looking surprised. 'Oh! You're still here, are you? Well, off you go, back on the train to Bristol. Tell them we make the ads, they make the sherry. 'Bye!'

For the most part, clients tolerated CDP's dismissive attitude. Most of them were small companies with only a limited budget to spend on advertising. CDP promised that their creative work would have massive impact regardless of expenditure. All they asked for in return was complete trust in their judgement. But it took the diplomacy of John Pearce and his account-handling department to maintain the delicate relationships. A key figure in this area was John Ritchie (who would later father the film-maker Guy Ritchie and, somewhat improbably, become Madonna's father-in-law). In the scruffy environs of CDP's offices, Ritchie stood out as a more old-fashioned adman. A former army officer with richly public school vowels, he had been in the business for some years. 'I'd been tramping the jungle in Malaysia during the war and quite enjoyed it,' he says.

> But once I left the army I didn't have a clue what I wanted to do. I went to meet an old friend at a pub called the Coach and Horses just off Berkeley Square. I didn't know it at the time but it was J Walter Thompson's local. I remember asking my friend, 'Who are all these people in here drinking and laughing in the middle of the afternoon?' He said, 'Oh, they work in advertising.' From that moment on I asked everyone I knew what advertising was and how I could get into it.

Ritchie was eventually employed by Charlie Lytle, an American businessman who owned the vast majority of advertising hoardings in London. 'He was eighteen stone,' recalls Ritchie.

During the war they'd had to drop him into Paris using two parachutes. He made me an account executive alongside a

Serbo-Croatian chap he'd employed in the army. Charlie had hired him as an assassin and he'd managed to kill eighteen Nazis for him. In return he gave him a job as an account man. The trouble was, he didn't speak a word of English and generally spoke to us in Ancient Greek.

After receiving this peculiar break into the industry, Ritchie eventually found himself as the respectable face of CDP's accounts department. 'There were a lot of maverick figures at Collett's so it was important to make sure the clients didn't feel too concerned,' he says. 'I would always try to skip out the marketing directors and speak straight to the chairmen or managing directors of any client. That way you could could get anything done.'

Even when they fell into serious debt, John Pearce refused to compromise the agency's strategy. When a famous cigarette company appointed the agency to launch their new brand in the early sixties, it seemed like a turning point. But the two parties were unable to agree on the correct brand strategy for the product and, eventually, Pearce wrote to the chairman resigning the business. 'I really do not think it sensible to continue to work for a client who will not accept the advice of his agency,' wrote Pearce. He also included a list of 'perfectly good agencies' whom he believed 'would not have that difficulty'.

Ritchie and others began to fear for the company's future but Pearce remained calm. He already had a raft of alcohol clients and told his troops: 'Where there's booze, fags will surely follow,' assuring them that other tobacco brands would soon present themselves. In the end they did, in the form of Gallaher, a then small tobacco firm based in Belfast. Their chairman, Tommy Ford, offered CDP the chance to handle their rather old-fashioned cigarette brand, Du Maurier. But John Pearce considered the product outdated and impossible to revive. He suggested that they instead handled their Benson and Hedges brand of king-size cigarettes, which Gallaher saw as having little potential. They agreed to let CDP handle its advertising but warned that they couldn't afford to spend much on it. 'Never mind the budget,' said Pearce. 'Give us the brand and we'll make something of it.' This was the turning point for CDP. They had found in Tommy Ford a client who was willing to lend them his entire trust. It was also an opportunity for the agency to make a splash in a medium they were yet to master: television.

'In the early years, CDP had been known as a visual agency,' says Alan Parker. 'They made these elegant-looking press ads with top photographers. But TV was really taking off and they hadn't proved themselves as an agency who could make stand-out commercials.' TV advertising was a fledgling medium that was looked down upon by those in the film industry. Some directors could be persuaded to work on commercials between film projects but would generally do so with a mild sense of shame.

'Because of the limitations of the directors who were around at that time, CDP decided to make the B&H commercials an extension of their successful press ads,' says Alan Parker. 'That way, they thought no one could really mess it up.' The press campaign had focused on the product's distinctive packaging, likening it to a precious object under the slogan 'Pure Gold'. When it came to making a television version, the agency decided to employ a stills photographer, Keith Ewert, as director. While film and television directors felt as if commercials were somehow below them, Ewert was appreciative of the opportunity and strove to achieve something original. The result was a striking ad in which a burglar's gloved hands were seen rummaging through a chest of valuables in search of the cigarette box. With Ewert's innovative lighting techniques and the improbable use of jazz music from the album *Jacques Loussier Plays Bach*, the commercial was an instant hit. Not only did it win awards but it helped set the brand on a course towards market domination. The trust between agency and client had been cemented and, over time, CDP would help Benson and Hedges go from unknown brand to the biggest-selling cigarette in the country. The commercial had raised the bar for television advertising. 'It was incredible and absolutely unusual,' says Alan Parker. 'It created a new visual style and a unique way of writing witty, thirty-second narratives. It gave the rest of us a sense for the first time that we could make ads that might be as good as, or better than, the programmes themselves.'

When Gallaher handed them the account for their cigar brand, Hamlet, CDP showed even greater ambition. Roy Carruthers and Tim Warriner, a creative team recently hired from New York, wrote a commercial in which a music teacher grew increasingly frustrated at his young pupil's cack-handed attempts at playing the piano. Eventually, the teacher lit a Hamlet cigar in order to soothe his nerves, at which point the pupil miraculously broke into a rendition of Bach's 'Air on a G String'. As the teacher's expression melted into blissful calm, the voice-over purred, 'Happiness is a cigar called Hamlet. The mild cigar'. The commercial served as a template for one of the UK's longest-running and most popular advertising campaigns.

Each advertisement featured ever more preposterous scenarios. A hapless golfer continuously fails to lift his ball out of the bunker; a tennis fan is prevented from following the ball across court by his neck brace; a bald man has his toupee inadvertently removed by his lover during a romantic meal. Each time, these simple set pieces would end with the same contemplative piece of music (which had originally been chosen by Colin Millward) and the familiar slogan. The campaign ran until 1991, ending only once the government banned tobacco advertising on television. Even then, the series of ads was released on a commemorative video. By that stage, CDP's campaign had long since transformed Hamlet from an obscure brand to the biggest-selling cigar in the UK. 'It is a classic example of a brand that was built through television advertising,' said Gallaher's Peter Wilson of the campaign.

While celebrities had appeared in commercials before, usually making sober endorsements of a product, CDP began to cast them as characters in comedic dramatisations. Peter Sellers and Spike Milligan played ham-fisted thieves in a Benson and Hedges commercial, while Peter Cook and Dudley Moore performed a musical number to advertise Harvey's Bristol Cream. Even the politician Clement Freud was used – as the unlikely face of Chunky dog food. 'We realised it was extremely effective,' says John Ritchie. 'I would sit at home and see a figure in a play or something and think to myself, He'd be perfect for our ad! Then we'd call them up and get them for relatively little money.'

Their flourishing knack for television helped CDP grow from a stylish but small agency into the hottest company in town. Their debts were gone, clients were banging on their door and the best creative talent in London flocked to work with them. They had become London's incarnation of Doyle Dane Bernbach. Meanwhile, DDB themselves were finally dipping a toe into the London advertising scene.

'I knew DDB had opened a London office in the autumn of 1964 but somehow I'd missed it happening,' says David Abbott, who was finding some success as a young copywriter with Mather and Crowther.

> I was very surprised when I opened a broadsheet newspaper one day and saw this ad, spread across two pages, for Remington shavers. It said, 'It Takes Guts To Charge £10 For A Razor' and showed all the separate parts of the razor next to a very naturalistic picture of an unshaved model. It was beautifully designed and defied most of the conventions of the time. That was a Damascus moment for me. I realised that, however well I was doing at Mather and Crowther, DDB was the only benchmark.

By 1965, Abbott had fulfilled his dream and moved into DDB's Baker Street offices. The creative department was being run by John Withers, a senior figure sent over from New York. The young British staffers were schooled in Bill Bernbach's techniques and instantly made an impact at the D&AD awards. In 1966, after their first full year of business, DDB London scooped the best television advertisement award for a Remington commercial. Written by John Withers, the ad pioneered a theme that would endure for decades: a man marvelled at the technical specifications of his shaver while an attendant young women cooed over his clean shave. That year, DDB had a total of fourteen advertisements in the D&AD annual, a figure bettered only by CDP with sixteen. 'It was a hard-working place where the pay was bad and the hours were long,' says Abbott. 'But it was considered an honour to work for them.'

Eventually, Abbott was sent to New York to learn Bernbach's methods at first hand. 'It was an intimidating experience,' he recalls.

The building was full of the industry's superstars. I remember being put on the Volkswagen campaign with an experienced art director called Hal. We had to come up with an idea for the Fastback sedan but it proved difficult and dragged on for about ten days. Eventually, my group head called me into his office and said, 'Hal wants you off the job because you're not solving the problem.' I said, 'We haven't been trying for that long!' But that was it. I was moved on to something less interesting. It was a humbling experience because back in London I'd been considered one of the best. It seemed the standards in New York were higher.

Back in London, DDB were struggling to maintain their success. Most of their early hits had been press ads for clients brought over from New York. They had failed to match CDP in the increasingly important area of television. And attracting new British clients proved difficult. 'DDB made two cardinal errors,' says John Salmon, who had joined as a copywriter in 1966. 'First, they sent a guy over from New York to run the place who was incredibly frugal. When I first joined he offered to take me out for lunch. But when the bill came he started to carefully work out what my share was! I said, "Don't bother, I'll pay for yours." He wasn't upset by that – he was pleased!'

Doyle Dane Bernbach had cultivated a sober image since their early days in New York. They wanted to stand out as a serious-minded, hard-working agency amid the prevailing opulence of the advertising industry. 'I had previously worked in New York, where the extravagance among most agencies was insane,' says Salmon.

Over at Young and Rubicam they had a top designer install a different architectural style on each floor. So on one floor it was American Colonial, on the next it was Bauhaus and on the next it was art nouveau. One creative director had his office decked out like the bridge of a ship. Another had an office like a barber's shop. But there was nothing like that at DDB – a fact which they celebrated.

The agency imposed a similarly austere regime in London. This did little to impress potential clients who visited their Baker Street HQ. 'This was a period in which agencies were starting to install bars in their offices,' says Salmon. 'It was the start of inflation and everyone was showing off. In that context, DDB looked relatively unsuccessful to visiting clients. We had Yale locks installed on individual offices because the building was so insecure.'

Creative struggles became a further problem for the agency. 'Bill Bernbach insisted on every piece of creative work being sent to New York for his approval,' says Salmon.

In one respect we were really flattered by this because, if your idea came back from New York with a tick from Bernbach, you knew you must have created something very special. But, really, it stopped us from infusing our ads with any Britishness. Bernbach had invented that colloquial style of writing in New York. I always thought they were going to apply the same style to British language and culture. There was so much to get hold of in Britain I thought it would be wonderful. But we couldn't do it.

Inevitably, Bernbach and his lieutenants failed to grasp the nuances of a British culture which, in the mid-sixties, was vastly different to that of America. 'I wrote a great script for Quaker Oats which was supposed to star Spike Milligan,' says Salmon.

It was set to go into production when, by chance, Bill Bernbach visited London for the week and happened to visit a show Milligan was doing in the West End called *Son of Oblomov*. It was entirely improvised so some nights it was funny and some nights it wasn't. Bernbach caught him on a bad night. He came into the office the next day and said, 'Does this Quaker commercial depend on this man Milligan? Well, he's not funny at all! I saw him last night!' And the ad was cancelled.

To make matters worse, DDB had a policy of not producing speculative work for clients. 'It was something they could get away with in New York because they had nothing to prove out there,' says David Abbott.

But in London, people wanted to see actual work before they handed over their marketing budget. Our attitude was: we'll tell you what our general philosophy is and show you the ads we've made for other people but we won't pretend to know your business inside out yet and we won't make it easy for you to hire us. Because of this, we found it very hard to attract new business. Especially as our competitors weren't so arrogant in their approach to clients.

Collett Dickenson Pearce were wowing viewers every night with their television commercials. Doyle Dane Bernbach simply couldn't keep up. 'It was largely a result of our clients' budgets,' says Abbott.

We didn't have a client like Chemstrad who could afford all that TV airtime. But it was also about the different talents of each agency. CDP had Colin Millward in charge, who was an art director, so they had a very visual tradition, whereas we focused more on producing strongly written press ads. In those early years about ninety-five per cent of our entries into the D&AD book were press ads while most of CDP's entries were TV.

Soon, DDB's most talented creatives were being drained by their greatest rivals. 'When I returned from New York, some of our star creatives had already moved to CDP,' says Abbott.

They paid a great deal more. Plus, it was a very different working culture. You heard these stories about CDP staff leaving cabs waiting for fifteen hours outside restaurants while they were getting pissed. But DDB was always slightly puritanical. That was Bernbach's aura and mine also. I never got pissed or into drugs or those sort of things. I was kind of, I suppose, faintly anal.

At CDP's Howland Street headquarters the most talented creatives in London were being assembled into a formidable team on the fourth floor. With its shabby office furniture, plastic-tiled flooring and peeling paintwork, it was hardly more glamorous than DDB. But when clients commented on the scruffiness of the creative department, John Pearce would tell them: 'We spend our money on salaries for the best people, not the decor. We believe they should have nice carpet on the floor in their homes. Not in the office.' And they did. 'The salaries were the highest in town; you couldn't earn more money,' says Alan Parker, who was made a creative head in his early twenties. 'John Pearce's philosophy was to give Colin [Millward] the maximum amount of money in order to hire the very best people in London. They poached everybody from DDB because they could offer them so much more pay.' John Salmon made the defection in 1967. 'They more than doubled my salary, that's why I joined them,' he says.

Millward and Pearce encouraged an atmosphere where people

could choose their own methods of working. An aura of chaos engulfed the ramshackle offices. When a young art director arrived in the office at eleven in the morning, Colin Millward called out from his office: 'You should have been here at nine thirty!' 'Why?' said the youngster. 'What happened at nine thirty?'

Impertinence, rudeness and lateness were tolerated at CDP. In return, Millward demanded that his staff push themselves to the limit in pursuit of creative excellence. 'The biggest lesson he taught me was that competence was a point of departure, not a point of arrival,' says David Puttnam.

The young men who occupied Howland Street's fourth floor were fast becoming the superstars of the industry. In the mid-sixties, the London *Evening Standard* ran an interview with Charles Saatchi, who, they reported, was the industry's highest-paid writer. The fresh-faced youth, who was still in his early twenties, was pictured sitting on the bonnet of his brand-new E-type Jaguar. It was the wider world's first depiction of advertising's growing affluence. 'The level of automotive excellence at CDP was quite amazing,' says John Salmon. 'There were twenty-one-year-olds driving around in Ferraris and Bentleys. When I arrived from DDB I told them I didn't need a car because I lived so near to the office. But they more or less forced me to get a Mercedes on the company!'

Decadent behaviour wasn't just tolerated, it was encouraged. 'The amount of drinking that went on was astonishing,' says Salmon. 'Pearce and Dickenson led by example. They were tipping down the Highland Pepsi in the office all day.' At a time when Doyle Dane Bernbach had made a stand against tobacco advertising, CDP appeared to have no ethical qualms about their business or personal conduct. 'Our biggest clients were booze and fags and we didn't really think about the morality of it all,' says Alan Parker. 'We were really too young to take that sort of thing into account. As for John Pearce, he was knocking back a bottle of Scotch and eighty fags a day so I don't suppose it occurred to him that he was part of anything immoral!' Pearce was no ordinary managing director. Parker remembers encountering his boss one evening on his way home. 'I'd left the pub and was on my way to the station when I saw John leaving the offices on Howland Street,' he says. 'I was about to say hello when he started to vomit profusely on to the pavement. Then he took out a handkerchief, wiped the corners of his mouth, brushed down the front of his Crombie and went on his way.'

As the sixties rolled on, CDP became a party that lasted all week long. Whether it was a lucrative piece of new business or another prestigious award, there was always something to celebrate. The agency had embarked upon a roll that would continue for more than twenty years. But while his underlings went wild with excitement, Colin Millward, the architect of the achievements, strove to maintain an air of grumpy reserve. 'It was an ambition of everyone's to get Colin to join in the party,' says Frank Lowe.

One day we managed it. We went to lunch at the Gay Hussar in Soho to celebrate winning a big new account. The drinking went on until six fifteen, at which point more people were flooding in for early suppers before the theatre. As we got up to leave we heard an almighty crash and turned to see Colin falling down the spiral staircase. This miserable Yorkshireman, who nobody had ever seen drunk before, lay there at the bottom of the stairs with blood pouring from his head and said: 'Well, Frank, I don't quite know what's happened here.' We'd finally got Millward drunk. It was the last mark of success we needed.

6

'For Mash Get Smash'

The product was Cresta soft drinks. The brief was infuriating in its simplicity: 'Tell everyone the taste story.' But conveying a taste sensation to a television audience was easier said than done. John Webster stared out of his office window in frustration. He thought about the movie he'd seen the night before, *Easy Rider*. A meandering, psychedelic drug romp featuring the wild-eyed antics of Dennis Hopper and Peter Fonda seemed an unlikely reference material for a soft drink commercial aimed at children. But there was one scene that kept coming back to him. Jack Nicholson makes a cameo as a young degenerate lawyer released from jail. In celebration, he takes out a bottle of Jim Beam and holds it aloft, declaring: 'Here's the first of the day, fellas! To old D. H. Lawrence.' Taking a sip, he starts to twitch violently, flapping one arm like a chicken while stuttering: 'Neh! Neh! Neh! Fuh! Fuh! Fuh! Indians!' Now there was a man telling the taste story, thought Webster. If he could get someone – or something – more suitable for his young audience to perform a similar routine, he might have cracked the brief. And so he wrote the story of the Cresta Bear, who lived in the North Pole but grew tired of drinking the salty seawater. He left his friends, family and homeland behind and embarked upon an obsessive search for something tastier. Eventually, he discovered Cresta and got hooked on the stuff. Each time he took a sip, he would launch into a series of involuntary spasms before exclaiming: 'It's frothy, man!' Webster had the bear created by animators and soon it was the star of a whole campaign of television commercials. Before long, playgrounds across the country were awash with children mimicking the bear's routine.

The 1973 campaign would serve as a breakthrough for both Webster and his employers, Boase Massimi Pollitt. Soon, he would establish a reputation as British advertising's great alchemist: a creative who could combine peer-pleasing creative panache with a resolutely populist appeal. The modest art director was on the verge of becoming the most successful British adman of them all. But things hadn't always run so smoothly. As the sixties drew to a close, John Webster felt as if he'd missed out on advertising's creative revolution. The best young admen of his generation were already making names for themselves at Collett Dickenson Pearce, Doyle Dane Bernbach or BBDO, the large agency that had just bought Papert Koenig and Lois. They were producing the kind of advertising Webster had always dreamed of. Meanwhile, he was in his mid-thirties, working as an art director at the comparatively stuffy Mather and Crowther. He lacked the flashiness and bravado of many of his contempories. He was a gangly, bespectacled figure possessed of a contemplative manner. His image was never likely to stand out amid adland's increasingly flamboyant glitterati. And his agency was hardly the place to be. 'I had a lot of energy and drive but my work wasn't in tune with the agency style,' he says. 'So I tiptoed my way through the work, deciding to keep it quite simple so as to not make any waves.'

There was only one place Webster really wanted to work. 'I wanted Colin Millward to call and offer me a job at CDP but he never did,' he says. 'DDB were doing work that was very American in its style. CDP was the first place to do stuff that was inherently British, which was really exciting. I was too proud to ring up and ask for a job there. I wanted to produce work so great that Millward would notice me. But I just couldn't get good-quality work through at Mather and Crowther.'

He was eventually offered an escape route by Hobson Bates. A large American agency, they weren't renowned for their creativity and hoped that the appointment of Webster might improve their reputation. But like many old-fashioned agencies at the time, their attempts to modernise were largely superficial. 'They basically used me as a performing monkey,' says Webster. 'They would wheel me out to clients with some piece of work that everybody knew they would never actually use and say, "This is what we could do!" Then they would show them a far safer idea which would always be the one that got used.'

Webster saw his chance of entering the industry's premier league slipping away even farther. 'I spent a year and a half there and realised that a creative person can't improve the standard of work on his own. You need all the departments in the agency, from the account executives to the financial department, working together to make a difference.' He managed to join Pritchard Wood Partners, a large agency owned by the American group Interpublic. It was here that he managed to produce his first piece of noteworthy work. 'It was a cinema ad for National Provincial Bank,' he recalls. 'It featured a little girl speaking directly to the audience. She delivered her speech brilliantly but what made it really funny was that she clearly needed to go the toilet throughout. She was wriggling about and it was really quite hilarious.' Unfortunately, Webster couldn't find a way of capturing the actress's comic discomfort in a thirty-second commercial and resigned himself to delivering a more prosaic version. But when a young account man, Frank Lowe, saw the longer cut he was overwhelmed. 'It was an extraordinary piece of work,' says Lowe. 'So unusual, as was most of the work John was producing there.' Lowe took it upon himself to make sure the public saw Webster's sixty-second version of the commercial. 'Half an hour after seeing it, Frank came back to me and said, "I've been on to the ad sales people at the cinemas and they say they'll run a sixty second-ad at no extra cost. No problem,"' recalls Webster. 'I remember thinking, now here's a real account man!' Thanks to Lowe's efforts, Webster's preferred version of the commercial ran in cinemas for several months, winning the admiration of the industry at large. Finally, Webster's star was in the ascendancy.

In 1968, three of Pritchard Wood's senior executives tried to purchase the agency from Interpublic. Martin Boase, Stanley Pollitt and Gabe Massimi approached the American owners with a generous offer but, when Interpublic hesitated on the deal, the trio decided to resign and form their own agency. 'I came into Pritchard Wood one morning to find that everyone seemed to be leaving to start a new agency and that I wasn't invited because I didn't have a client to take with me,' remembers Frank Lowe. 'I was furious!'

Boase Massimi Pollitt opened the doors of their small Goodge Street offices in 1968. John Webster nearly didn't join. 'David Abbott was trying to woo me into joining DDB at the time,' he recalls. 'Suddenly, there was a sense of real opportunity in my career. But BMP seemed a good chance to start something really exciting.'

BMP's founders identified a gap in the advertising market. 'We saw agencies that produced very interesting and original work with absolutely no sound foundation and other agencies that produced work that was soundly based but extremely dreary,' says Martin Boase, the agency's founding managing director. 'We thought there was a road between the two whereby we could make brilliantly creative advertising that was based on extremely sound strategy.' It was a boom time for British advertising and several new agencies were starting up with outlandish statements of intent. Martin Boase understood the importance of standing out from the crowd. 'It was unusual for ad agencies to court the press in those days,' he says. 'But I cultivated relationships with the trade magazines and even managed to get a whole-page article in the *Sunday Times*, detailing the drama of the breakaway from Pritchard Wood.' Boase looked at every angle possible to gain publicity for his fledgling agency; he even courted the Conservative cabinet minister Ernest Marples to join as chairman. 'He refused at first but I wrote him a long handwritten letter and delivered it myself to his home in Belgravia,' he says. 'He eventually came on board and we announced the appointment on ticker-tape in Piccadilly Circus. We had to get rid of him after a couple of years because he would rarely turn up to meetings but by then he'd served his purpose.'

Boase issued his staff with a fleet of brown Minis bearing the company logo. 'All the other agencies gave their staff flashy sports cars,' says John Webster. 'But we got a tremendous amount of publicity driving around town in these Minis. It also made us seem very fashionable.' Long before advertising agencies employed their own publicity departments, Boase was cultivating a strong public identity for BMP. 'I saw the blank side of a company car as wasted ad space,' he explains. The agency was equally innovative in the way it treated staff. 'We spread shares throughout the whole company,' says Boase. 'Even Pat the tea lady was given some, and when we finally went public in the eighties she made about thirty grand from them.' The agency strove to be non-hierarchical and the offices were open plan. In the late sixties, BMP set a template for trendily casual working environments that would later become an ad agency cliché.

The agency felt certain they could produce work with both creative flair and strategic credibility. Central to this was Stanley Pollitt, their small, scruffy account executive, who possessed a fascination with research. Pollitt had begun his career in advertising in the media department at Pritchard Wood before becoming a creative and then an account man. Eventually, he became a board member with special responsibility for research. His experience of different advertising disciplines gave him a unique insight into the business. He realised that the account and creative departments would often work at cross-purposes. While the creatives tried to make ads to please themselves and their peers, account executives would encourage work that slavishly pandered to clients. Pollitt believed that all advertising should be made with the consumer in mind. He believed that the use of effective research methods could inform creative work that pleased everyone: from egotistical copywriters and designers to jittery clients. He established a 'planning department' at BMP, which would become central to all the agency's work. It would, he insisted, represent the consumer throughout the whole development process of an ad campaign. Through careful research and analysis, it would work out why people responded to certain advertisements and not others. This would provide the creative department with invaluable information on which to build their ideas. It would also reassure clients that the ads were supported by rational thinking and rigorous strategy.

Pollitt was an unlikely advertising guru. He had been educated at Oxford, where, despite his small stature, he had been an accomplished boxer. He had turned his back on a planned career as a barrister to become an adman and had taken to it instantly. But his success had little to do with charisma or charm. He was renowned for his appalling dress sense and terrible presentation skills. Like a bumbling professor, he would mumble his way through client meetings, often turning his back on the audience. He would lose his notes and often his temper, allegedly utilising his boxing skills in the boardroom when decisions didn't go his way. Martin Boase once had to lock him in his office to prevent him from attending a particularly sensitive client meeting. He was never without a cigarette in mouth or, after lunch, a glass of wine in his hand. But despite his eccentricities, Pollitt's ideas helped drive BMP. The entire agency was built around his innovative thoughts on strategic planning (a term he appropriated from JWT's Stephen King, the other great thinker in this field). 'Planning can only work when there is a total agency commitment to getting the advertising content right at all costs,' he said. 'Getting it right being more important than maximising agency profits, than keeping clients happy or building an agency shop window for distinctive-looking advertising.'

For most creatives, this method of working was anathema. 'Planning is just a posh word for saying "let's find out what the punters think",' says former BMP creative Dave Trott. 'Most creatives wouldn't touch it with a bargepole. They'd say, "Why are you asking twelve housewives what they think of *my* work?"' But, in John Webster, BMP had unearthed a creative figure who was only too happy to embrace the directives of the planning department. 'He was absolutely not interested in what the advertising fraternity thought,' says Trott. 'They weren't as good as him anyway, so why would he give a shit what they thought? He was interested in what the bloke in the street thought. He knew his job was to motivate and manipulate that bloke in the street. That was why he was perfect for planners to work with.'

For the first three years, BMP's creative department was under the control of Gabe Massimi. A flamboyant American with a high industry profile, he helped earn the agency early publicity. Webster, meanwhile, was happy to serve as his modest apprentice. 'He was a very good-looking bloke who enjoyed the lifestyle that went with the job,' says Webster. 'He used to come in about four in the afternoon smelling of aftershave, freshly showered, park his Porsche and ask me what was going on. I had to brief him just before he went into any important meetings.' Massimi's flair mixed well with Webster's more studious approach – but eventually things came to a head. 'The agency was still young and going through a rough time in 1971,' says Boase. 'We had to make economies and so we fired Massimi. At the time he seemed to think we couldn't possibly survive without him but that's not how it turned out.' It quickly became clear to the partners that their creative success had been courtesy of John Webster, not Gabe Massimi. Never was this more apparent than when the agency were asked to advertise Cadbury's instant potato product, Smash. 'Massimi came up with a campaign idea based around the slogan "English Girls Are Smashing",' recalls Boase. 'Meanwhile, Webster had come up with his own ideas that we felt were much better.'

In the early seventies, convenience foods were becoming big business. But it was widely assumed that intelligent advertising was redundant in this market. 'Packaged goods were the biggest spenders on advertising, had the most sophisticated marketing people and generally made the dreariest advertising,' says Martin Boase. 'It was a widely accepted rule that their accounts would only go to big agencies. We sought to break that rule.'

Webster resolved to find a new approach for Smash. Instead of referring to the pseudo-scientific market research that was widely applied to the grocery market, he utilised Stanley Pollitt's more impressionistic research. 'We found that housewives were bored stiff with adverts featuring other housewives,' he says.

> One night, I was in the pub with my copywriter Chris Wilkins and I said to him: 'It's crazy! If anyone came down from another planet and saw that we bothered to peel potatoes, boil them and mash them up when you can just get it out of a packet, they'd think we were barmy!' When I came in the next morning Chris had written this up into a script and so I drew up some pictures. We showed it to the client but they thought we were barmy. I just asked them to put it into the research with a bunch of other ideas and, of course, the housewives loved it. Cadbury's were forced into running the commercial.

The original advertisement proclaimed 'Cadbury's Smash has a serious rival!' Over a simple film of the product, a voice-over explained that the competitive product was hard, round and knobbly and required peeling, boiling and mashing. 'It's good,' quipped the end line. 'But it will never catch on.' Soon after the commercial was made, Gabe Massimi left the agency and Webster was appointed creative director.

Webster began to elaborate on his idea. He wrote a script about a group of tin-headed Martians on board their spaceship. 'On your last trip did you discover what the earth people eat?' asked their leader.

'They eat a great many of these,' responded one of his lieutenants, holding up a potato between his robotic pincers. 'They peel them with their metal knives. They boil them for twenty of their minutes, then they smash them to pieces!' he explained.

'They clearly are a most primitive people!' observed the leader, while his crew descended into hysterics.

Webster hired the American Bob Brooks to direct the commercial. Brooks had quit his career as a successful creative director with Benton and Bowles in the late sixties to become a photographer before turning to directing. Despite his notorious bad temper, comedy had become his speciality. 'I arrived on set and saw these little tin robots,' he remembers. 'And I worked out that I wanted to shoot them like real actors. I wanted them to talk and react to one another like humans would. So I decided to imagine that they were real people just wearing tin heads.' In reality, a stage had been built four feet high so that a team of puppeteers could sit below, manipulating the Martians. Brooks, however, refused to acknowledge the existence of the men sitting below. 'We started to shoot the commercial and there was this one fucking robot who kept doing the wrong thing,' he says. 'So I went and started shouting at the damn thing knowing full well that the guy underneath would be getting the message.' Webster was astounded by the director's behaviour. 'He went berserk at this Martian, which was basically an inanimate object,' he recalls. 'He had to be held back from beating the thing up.' Brooks was certain that his approach would lend the ad comic realism. '*Thunderbirds* was a popular TV show at the time but they just filmed them in a flat way that didn't attempt to disguise the fact that they were puppets,' he says. 'But I filmed the Smash Martians as if they were human, shooting full focus and at interesting angles.' The commercial's most popular moment occurred by mistake in the closing minutes of filming. 'On the final take, as they were all supposed to be laughing, one of these fucking Martians fell over sideways. It was an accident but, when it came to the edit, I realised it looked pretty funny. As if he were falling over laughing. So I left it in.'

The behaviour of the Martians proved infectious with audiences. Cadbury's had only planned the commercial as a one-off but ended up running it as a campaign for over a decade. In 2005, a national poll to celebrate fifty years of commercial television advertising saw Smash voted the most popular campaign of all time. 'I made hundreds of commercials plus a couple of feature films,' says Brooks. 'But whenever I tell people about the stuff I've made, they're always most interested in those Smash commercials. I don't understand why. I do know that kids adored the ads and that when they saw them they would say, "Hey, Mum, I want some Smash! And mums would buy Smash." '

The commercial was a hit at the following year's D&AD awards, cementing BMP's reputation as one of the leading agencies in town. Despite his central role in their meteoric rise to prominence, Webster never requested that his name be put on the agency's door. 'I had some shares in the company which I'd bought when I joined, which was enough,' he says. While the rest of the industry had embraced the pairing up of copywriters and art directors as creative teams, Webster increasingly preferred working alone. Although ostensibly an art director, he conceived fully rounded ideas such as the Cresta Bear with immense detail. Such ideas were born out of an imagined world that existed only in his mind and defied collaboration. He was a rare example of a creative who was often credited as both the art director and copywriter on his adverts. But he was hardly a recluse and would nurture the talent of younger creatives with great enthusiasm. BMP's reputation was growing and numerous aspiring admen flocked there to learn from Webster. 'In the early seventies, we had two per cent of the entire graduate population in Britain apply to BMP,' says Boase. 'We worked out that we spent the equivalent of an account executive's annual salary just going through the recruitment process.'

Dave Trott applied for a job at BMP after arriving back from New York in the early seventies. 'I knew there was a job for me somewhere in advertising,' says Trott. 'But I couldn't be bothered dragging my book round to agencies having interviews with people who weren't as good as me at the job. I wasn't the best but, to be fair, I knew I was in the top five or ten per cent.' The young creative photocopied examples of his work and sent them out to fifty advertising agencies picked at random from the Yellow Pages. The majority rejected him but Webster invited him in for an interview. 'I showed him my work, most of which was stuff I'd done at college. Admittedly, some of it was ripped off from other people. But only the stuff I knew I could have easily done anyway. I mean, it would have been really dopey to have nicked stuff I knew I couldn't have done!' Trott was hired and quickly established himself as a young star of the agency. After six months, he was offered a full-time job by Webster. After accepting, the young creative excitedly confessed to his mentor that his original portfolio had contained work stolen from other people. The usually docile Webster was unimpressed. 'He went ballistic!' recalls Trott.

BMP was revelling in its new lofty status. By the mid-seventies it was the only rival to CDP at the annual award ceremonies. Its new offices in Paddington were occupied by a young team who gleefully embraced the decadent adland lifestyle. 'There was a nearby pub called the Prince of Wales which was always known as the POW,' recalls Dave Trott.

We used to be there from eleven in the morning until three in the afternoon, which was when pubs used to shut. We'd then get a cab over to Harrods because their off-licence was the only place you could buy a drink after three. We'd bring a couple of bottles of tequila back, get smashed and roll a couple of joints until the pubs opened again at seven. Then we'd stay there until they shut again at eleven.

Despite such excess, John Webster ensured that BMP's productivity never suffered. 'We often felt like a one-man team,' says Trott. 'John wasn't very hedonistic. Week in, week out, he was like the player on the football team who was always man of the match. Occasionally one of us would sober up for long enough to score a goal.'

BMP's creative staff were certain that their rivals were in a worse condition. 'However bad we got we always knew we could do more work than the people at other agencies because they didn't seem to be doing any work at all,' says Trott. 'At CDP they were drunk all the time. They'd do one award-winning ad then spend the next eleven months in the pub. Whereas I would write four or five ads in the morning before the pubs opened.'

Webster was happy in his role as an amused spectator. 'It was a wonderful time, certainly the best few years of my life,' he reflects.

> We all felt as if we were at the centre of something. One of my writers, Gray Jolliffe, told me that he propositioned every single girl he ever met. It was a numbers game to him. Even if he only succeeded in seducing two per cent of them, he would still have had more women than the rest of us. I used to sit in an office with him and he'd see a pretty girl walking past the window. So he'd quickly write 'Fancy a coffee later?' on a piece of card and hold it up to the glass. Very often they'd say yes.

Webster also found time to nurture the creative talent of his young staff. 'I had this idea for Pepsi,' remembers Dave Trott.

> It was a slogan that said literally everything about the drink in one line: 'Lipsmackingthirstquenchingacetastinmotivatingoodbuzzin-cooltalkinhighwalkinfastlivinevergivincoolfizzin Pepsi.' I'd taken the idea from a Tom Wolfe book that was popular at the time called *Kandy-Kolored Tangerine-Flake Streamline Baby*. And then I got a DJ from a pirate radio station to read it out in a really fast, distinctive way. I said to John: 'I don't think it will research very well

because people aren't used to such long slogans that fill up the whole screen. But he said, 'Yeah, but that's what's great about it – it's unusual.' And he pushed the whole thing through.

The proto-rap style in which the slogan was delivered helped immediately establish Pepsi as the hip alternative to Coca-Cola in the mid-seventies.

Meanwhile, Webster was churning out his own successful ideas at a prolific rate. He made a series of award-winning advertisements for Courage beers under the slogan 'It's what your right arm's for'. He created a campaign for Unigate Dairies surrounding the Humphreys: a breed of never-seen, fantastical creatures which were alleged to steal milk from doorsteps. The commercials featured the likes of Muhammad Ali and Spike Milligan singing rhymes and warning, 'Watch out, there's a Humphrey about!'

Next came the Cresta Bear. It was a campaign so successful that other clients demanded imitations. 'After Cresta they would all call and say, "Can you invent something for us? We love the idea of a product character,"' says Webster. He was happy to indulge them. 'At that point in time there were a few brands who had their own characters. Like the PG Tips chimps and the Homepride Men,' he says.

> But increasingly, people were using celebrities. Famously, CDP had used Leonard Rossiter for their Cinzano campaign. I'd heard that most people in research thought that the ads were for Martini so I realised a celebrity could be a distraction from the product. But if we invented our own characters then we could own them. Plus, they wouldn't age and they'd be a great deal cheaper too.

When Sugar Puffs hired BMP to market their cereal, it seemed the perfect opportunity to create such a character. 'They wanted us to advertise it to kids in a way that would appeal to mums too,' says Webster. 'So the strategy was to emphasise the fact that it was flavoured with honey, not sugar. It gave it a more natural image.'

During visits to America, Webster had seen *The Andy Williams Show*, a TV variety showcase hosted by the popular lounge-style singer. One of the recurring comedy characters on the programme was the Cookie Bear, a gangly figure in a bear suit whose escapades would drive Williams to heated distraction. 'This creature would bang on the door halfway through the show and shout, "Cookies! I want cookies!" ' says Webster. 'And Williams would tell him he never wanted to see him again, "Not now, not ever NEVER!" I thought it was a very funny idea.' Webster imagined a similar creature with an obsessive predilection for honey.

> I wrote this story which explained that, in the earliest days on earth, there lived a breed of animal on the coast of Africa called the Honey Midgets. They lived on nothing but honey. One day, a few of them escaped their home on a log and washed up on a faraway island. There was honey being made by bees on this island but it was all high up in the trees. The midgets couldn't reach it but, after years of stretching, they evolved into giant creatures called Honey Monsters. One day, a character played by [the well-known television actor] Henry McGee went over to the island with the navy and brought one of these monsters back as a souvenir. It lived with Henry in England and believed him to be his mother. Hence the catchphrase 'Tell 'em about the honey, Mummy!'

Webster was certain that such elaborate backstories were fundamental to a successful campaign. 'With all the characters I invented I liked to imagine where they had come from and what their upbringing was like so that they'd be real, rounded characters as opposed to filmsy advertising mascots.' It proved successful. In theory, the premise for the campaign seemed faintly absurd. In practice, a series of commercials featuring a domestic arrangement between a slightly camp, middle-aged man and a giant, cereal-devouring yellow monster was rather surreal. But BMP's thorough planning and research techniques allayed any fears the client may have had.

The outlandish idea became a successful campaign that ran for almost three decades. Sugar Puffs even published Webster's Honey Monster biography and gave it away as a free gift with boxes of cereal. Sales rocketed.

BMP were making a name for themselves as the masters of mass-market advertising. Products such as Cresta and Sugar Puffs were aimed squarely at the housewives of Britain but Webster proved that they could be advertised with clever, thoughtful ideas. 'If you look at the famous CDP campaigns during the same period, they were all pretty middle class,' he says. 'Products like Benson and Hedges, Hamlet, Harvey's Bristol Cream and even Birds Eye were relatively sophisticated. But by chance we got the mass-market stuff and managed to make that our forte.'

By the mid-seventies, Webster's work had helped advertising earn a new cultural recognition. The early efforts of CDP and its peers had proved that the ad industry could produce slick work with impressive production values. Within an industry increasingly prone to navel-gazing, their work had set the standard. But in the eyes of the wider world advertising still lacked cultural credibility. Webster and his colleagues believed their work should demand the same respect as music, film or art, while the public saw the ad break as a garish irritant. 'We took our work very seriously and for many years no one else seemed to,' he says. 'It was frustrating in the early days.' Webster was sensitive to the wider world's perception of his business, explaining in the 1976 D&AD annual: 'It's being at a party when someone asks you what you do for a living and you're pleased to tell them, instead of cupping your mouth with your hand like you've got halitosis and whispering, "Advertising."' Through the humanity and humour of his work, the shy adman convinced the public that the ad break was actually worth looking forward to. And he'd even managed to earn advertising a modicum of respect.

7

'Your Daily Bread'

It was late and the crew were flagging. They'd been shooting a test commercial for Benson and Hedges' small cigars for over twelve hours. A test commercial that was unlikely to ever see the light of day. But that didn't seem to matter to the director. As far as he was concerned, no one was leaving before he'd got every last detail right. John Salmon, the seasoned creative who had written the script, looked at him in astonishment. 'He was standing in the middle of the set with a camera attached to his head, two black eyes and a bloodied lip,' he recalls. 'He refused to quit. I knew then that I would have to shoot him to stop him.'

No one had seen anyone work like this before. In the late sixties, one director was on a mission to revolutionise the way in which adverts were made. His name might not have been famous yet but his tenacity, talent and rampant ambition would soon make him one of the industry's biggest stars. Ridley Scott was about to change everything.

'The ad was only a little experiment really,' says Salmon, the creative head from Collett Dickenson Pearce. 'Gallaher dreamt up a small cigar that was shaped like a cigarette. They asked us to knock up a test advertisement but we knew it was unlikely to ever amount to much.'

The script described a burglar breaking into a house in search of a packet of the small cigars. As it was only a non-broadcast test, CDP hadn't paid close attention to the project. They hired a cheap studio in Chiswick that was ordinarily used for pornographic movies. And rather than hire one of their preferred directors, they used Ridley Scott, the wiry North-Easterner with long, reddish-blond hair and a notoriously intense manner.

'When we arrived at the studio, nothing was ready,' says Salmon. 'They'd been shooting a "sexual education" film overnight and the place was a mess. Plus, it was much bigger than we needed, which could have caused major problems. But Ridley seemed to work round everything.' The script required everything to be filmed from the burglar's point of view as he moved silently through the house. When shooting got under way, Salmon was amazed to discover the director's creative solution to this tricky brief. 'He had built a special rig and attached a camera to his head,' he says.

> He would climb through the window and move around the house as if he were the burglar. He had two assistants on either side of him playing his left and right hands respectively, so we could see them rifling through things looking for the cigars. He got a third assistant to run along beside them adjusting the lens with a special stick. It was remarkable to behold.

Scott was adamant that the whole script could be conveyed in a single shot. He would have to move quickly across the unexpectedly large set in order to fit all the action into thirty seconds. 'He ran through the first take shouting instructions at this team as he went,' says Salmon. 'The guy pulling the lens kept bashing him in the face with his stick and the guys playing the hands were struggling to keep up. At the end of the first take he already had a black eye. Then he started it all over again. I was staggered by his level of commitment to this piddling little commercial.'

British advertising had been waiting for a figure like Scott for some time. A generation of writers and art directors had elevated the standard of creative ideas but were unable to find directors who could properly execute their scripts. 'At Collett Dickenson Pearce we spent a great deal of time and money trying to improve the quality of images in our press and poster ads,' says Salmon. 'We would hire the best photographers and utilise the best technology to finesse the pictures afterwards. We tried to take the same attitude into TV advertising but it was tougher because the specialists didn't exist.' In the early years of TV advertising, agencies turned to film or television directors. 'If you look at British movies from that period, they weren't lit very well at all. They were always quite flat and the shadows crossed. It was a pretty generic look that tried to mimic Hollywood films of the time.'

Advertising imagery in the press had been revolutionised by a generation of photographers such as David Bailey, Terence Donovan, Brian Duffy and David Montgomery. They had found a way of presenting the most mundane consumer products as objects of tantalising beauty. But it was proving difficult to repeat the trick on television. 'Eventually, we started asking stills photographers to light our television shoots,' says Salmon. 'But we were in the grip of the unions, who disapproved. In the end, we would pay a union-registered lighting cameraman to stay at home and pay a photographer separately to come to the shoot and light everything.'

People who actually referred to themselves as full-time ad directors were few and far between. And those who did were yet to develop the sort of enthusiasm for making ads that was displayed by ad agency creatives. Without the technical experts to properly execute their ideas, the masterminds of advertising's creative revolution had hit a plateau. 'By the late sixties we'd made great strides,' says Salmon. 'But the technical people were still trying to catch up.' Then came Ridley Scott.

Ridley Scott was born in South Shields in 1937. 'My dad served in the Second World War then afterwards we all moved to Germany when he was sent there as part of the clean-up,' he says. 'I constantly changed schools throughout my childhood before ending up back in the North-East. But the travel was good education.' His older brother Frank enrolled in the merchant navy but Scott had no interest in following in his father or brother's adventurous footsteps. Once the family settled in Teesside, he enrolled at the West Hartlepool College of Art and graduated in 1958 with a diploma in design. He progressed to an MA in graphic design at London's Royal College of Art, where he contributed to the student magazine, *Ark*, and helped establish the film department. As part of his final show, he made a short film entitled *Boy on a Bicycle* starring his parents and younger brother Tony. 'It was actually pretty good,' he recalls.

Scott had a stellar reputation at the RCA. His final show earned him a job offer from the BBC as a designer. But he chose to defer his career in favour of visiting the United States. He spent nine months travelling on a Greyhound bus, eventually arriving in New York. 'I had started to become very interested in fashion while at college and loved the work of New York fashion designers,' he says. 'Just by saying I was an RCA graduate from London I managed to get meetings with a lot of them. There was a pro-British feeling there among fashion people at the time.' Soon he had secured a meeting with one of his greatest heroes. 'I went to see Bert Stern at his office in Lexington Street,' he says. 'He was a big deal and I remember showing him my portfolio over a hamburger. He already had an assistant but promised me a job if I came back a year later. I think he would have given it to me too.'

A talented photographer, illustrator and film-maker, Scott was unsure which discipline should form the basis of his career. In his mid-twenties, his priorities weren't entirely artistic. 'I liked fashion because it was exciting and full of girls,' he says.

> Bert invited me out to dinner with a couple of models and told me, 'I've got another Brit coming out this evening too.' It turned out to be David Bailey. I was only a kid and couldn't believe I'd managed to talk myself into this situation. Years later, Bailey was working for my production company and I asked him if he remembered that evening in New York. He said he didn't and I wasn't surprised because he'd been completely smashed!

The young graduate was driven by an unquenchable ambition. During his time in New York, he managed to involve himself with some of the city's most talented creative figures. 'It was force of will,' he explains. 'I wanted to get on and so I was completely relentless with people.' Soon, he was infiltrating the film industry. 'I sought out this pair of brilliant documentary makers called Richard Leacock and D. A. Pennebaker,' he says.

> They were very arty and innovative and I decided to wait for them in the lobby of their building. I knew they would walk through every day between nine and eleven so once they appeared I started talking to them and followed them all the way up in the lift. By the time we got to their floor they'd invited me in for a coffee and an hour later they'd offered me a job.

Scott worked for the pair for several months before returning to the UK to take up his job at the BBC. 'They'd kept the position open for me and I went in at quite a high level with my own assistant and everything,' he says.

> I was immediately working as a set designer on high-profile shows like *Dick Emery* and a programme called *Marriage Lines* with Prunella Scales. I was good at my job but I was a nuisance

because I was always moaning about things. The bureaucracy at the BBC was insane and nothing could be done without the decision going through numerous levels. In the end, I think to keep me happy and out of their hair, they asked me if I wanted to take a four-month production course and I said yes.

Scott's first directing experience came on BBC series such as *Z Cars* and *Adam Adamant Lives*. It seemed that his career had finally found focus – but he was pursuing a lucrative new sideline. Each day, after finishing work at his BBC offices in White City, he would climb into his white Mini and drive straight to Chelsea. The car had been a £250 investment; it was the only way he could shuttle between his two jobs. His destination was the home-cum-studio of Keith Ewert, Britain's hottest new commercials director. 'I'd got into it when a freelance designer at the BBC had asked me to cover for her on an ad she couldn't do,' says Scott. 'I thought it wasn't worth risking my job by moonlighting. Then she told me how much I would get paid.'

Inside Ewert's studio, Scott found the director and his team gathered round a chest of valuables, filming the soon-to-be-famous Gold Box commercial for Benson and Hedges. Scott may have gone there for the money but he stayed to learn more about the craft. 'Keith was making really quite beautiful ads,' he says.

He copied a lot of lighting techniques from the American photographer Irving Penn. In that sense he was one of the first ad directors to actually take the medium seriously and try to innovate. I designed some of his ads but he would eventually get annoyed with my questions and tell me to bugger off. But I would say, 'I don't want to bugger off, I want to stay and watch.' So he'd let me stay and I would learn about lighting.

Despite his rising status as a respected director at the BBC, Scott was dissatisifed with the job. 'They eventually gave me a live show to

93

direct called *Softly Softly* and even a short film. But it was a lot of responsibility for not much money and the ads were really taking off.'

Again, Scott's tenacity was paying off. What had started as a one-off favour for a friend had quickly turned into a full-time occupation. He cultivated his relationship with Ewert and the admen who visited the set. In his first year, he managed to make one hundred ads while still holding down his BBC job. 'Ridley could be very shy,' says Graham Terry, the ad agency producer who commissioned much of Keith Ewert's work. 'He was this young lad who'd come in and build the most amazing sets you'd ever seen. But if you complimented him on them, he'd blush.' Terry hired Ewert to make a series of Fairy Liquid commercials for his agency, KMP. The popular ads always featured a mother and daughter washing dishes and ended with the slogan: 'Now hands that do dishes can be soft as your face, with mild green Fairy Liquid.' It was the sort of conventional campaign that the trendier agencies might have sneered at but Ewert's lighting techniques and Scott's design ideas lent them a rare aesthetic quality. 'They were beautiful commercials,' Scott asserts.

Graham Terry was impressed by Scott's visual sensibilities and his perfectionism on set. With specialist ad directors a rare commodity, he thought he could make one out of the young set designer. 'We had a very simple, short script for Regent Petrol,' he says. 'The idea was to have a cowgirl with a petrol pump in her holster. I just wanted really strong imagery and it was clear Ridley could do that sort of stuff with his eyes closed.'

Scott remembers being approached by the agency man. 'One day Graham said to me, "Have you ever thought about directing an ad?" And I said, "Every day!" I'd seen how autonomous Keith was on set. What he said went, even down to the type of coffee we drank. I loved that – it was such a contrast to the bureaucracy of the BBC.'

Soon, Scott was offered representation as an ad director by a small Soho production company run by Peter Simms. 'They were smart to have spotted me so early,' he says.

The money I was making out of ads per day was four times what I could have earned at the BBC and I worked out that as an ad designer and sometime director I could maybe shoot over one hundred days per year. I had a strong financial and business head even back then and thought to myself, Something's up here!

In mid-sixties Britain, quitting a full-time job in favour of a freelance career in a fledgling industry was not the done thing. Scott recalls: 'I'd just bought our first house in East Sheen and we had one son with another on the way. But I thought quitting the BBC was a gamble that could pay off. When my father found out he couldn't believe it. He said: "What are you going freelance for? You've got a job!"'

Scott's unapologetic pursuit of money was unusual. While his sixties contemporaries spoke of fulfilling their creative ambitions and overthrowing the old guard, Scott was more pragmatic. But his financial motivations only served to fuel his pursuit of creative excellence. He quickly decided that the best route to economic success was to be the best at what he did.

'When I started, the industry was still a bit depressed,' he says.

But I could see that it was a light bulb that was about to shine a light on the rest of culture and society. I could see that the way society was going, with consumerism and so on, advertising was going to become a driving force. I could see it was the way that the whole world was going. I got that and that was what got me to decide to take it very seriously. I decided to elevate the medium.

Scott's visual style had an immediate impact on the industry. He was embraced by traditional agencies that were keen to lend artistic flair to their prosaic scripts. In a basement studio in Soho's Wardour Street, he filmed a series of commercials for Radion soap powder with a visual finesse that was unprecedented. 'I copied the greats,' he says.

I would take Orson Welles as my inspiration for lighting a soap powder ad in a kitchen. I would study something he'd done in *Citizen Kane* then try to recreate it the next day on set. It was all about trying to make these things that people had previously seen as insignificant little commercials into mini-movies. Because I got that ads were going to be massive.

This approach saw his credibility rocket among agencies and clients alike. He was a troubleshooter for bland advertising; someone who could transform dull ideas into visually striking epics. 'He wasn't fashionable among the cognoscenti at CDP and BMP,' says Sid Roberson. 'But he was loved by lots of good agencies because you could give him any crap idea and he would turn it into some masterpiece. He was totally brilliant.'

By the early seventies, Roberson had quit his work as an art director and was starting out as a photographer. His friendship with Scott soon provided an improbable sideline. 'Ogilvy and Mather hired me to shoot a Strongbow cider commercial,' says Scott.

I needed to find someone to play Mr Strongbow, who needed to be this strapping Viking character. I couldn't find the right bloke so in the end I asked Sid. He had been Mr UK and had the blond hair and good looks and I thought he'd be perfect. At first he said, 'Leave it out, Ridley!' But I told him he'd get paid the same day rate as he got as a photographer and eventually convinced him to do it.

On the first day of filming, Roberson stood astride the battlements of a castle on the Isle of Skye dressed in full Viking regalia, waiting for instructions from his friend Ridley Scott. 'In those days, he was terrible with actors,' recalls Roberson. 'He saw them as props. He would just shout stuff like "Left arm up a bit, right arm down a bit". After about the fourteenth take I was starting to feel like a useless piece of shit, but he didn't care. All he wanted to do was get his frame right.'

For the commercial's final scenes, Roberson was filmed drinking pints of Strongbow in a studio. 'I barely drank in those days so I asked them to fake the pints using tea or something,' he says.

But they wouldn't so I ended up having to drink four or five pints of this stuff. I'd managed to pull this model who was working in the same studios and was supposed to be sharing a cab home with her. Of course, once I climbed into the back seat with her I was wasted. She said, 'You're drunk!' and I threw up in her lap.

Despite early calamities, Roberson and Scott made several more Strongbow commercials together. 'Sid became known in the street as Mr Strongbow,' laughs Scott. 'He got loads of fan mail from housewives and everything.' But Roberson wanted to be more than a cider-drinking sex symbol. His photography was flourishing and he saw directing as the next step. He used his time on set with Scott as his education. 'He would get me to do the scariest things,' he says. 'I would be perched on the top of this castle wall with no support, being a total coward. Then I'd hear Ridley shout, "Action!" and I'd think, "Where is he?" Then I'd see him hanging from a parapet by his fingertips just to get the right shot.'

Scott combined his physical bravery with a painter's eye for detail. 'I once hired him to make a Heinz commercial set in a prison cell,' says Graham Terry. 'He told the prop man that he wanted a tin pot to be under the bed with a royal coat of arms on it. The prop man told him he couldn't source one in time. So Ridley took a plain pot and hand-painted a perfect coat of arms on it there and then on the set. It was amazing.'

Scott obsessively taught himself every film-making discipline and worked relentlessly. 'He was completely driven and focused,' says Roberson. 'He would shoot for hours and hours. It was a nightmare for the crew and actors. He was the best cinematographer, the best camera operator, the best designer out of anybody there.'

97

The ad industry had finally found their specialist director. Scott was changing the criteria by which commercials would be judged. The aesthetic qualities of his commercials were superior to anything seen in TV programmes or feature films at the time. Agencies clamoured to hire him. 'Prior to Ridley, there had been a production company in Soho called Television Advertising that represented a string of feature film directors,' says Graham Terry.

> But they were the types who you'd hire to make a biscuit commercial and they'd say, 'I'm a creative genius, I'll make you a great ad, don't tell me to do a close-up of the product!' But Ridley knew how to move the medium on. He understood marketing as well as film-making. After all, we were trying to make commercials, not art films.

Not that Scott was a slave to the will of his clients. 'He wasn't a prima donna,' says Roberson. 'Most directors would go mad if a client or someone from the agency tried to tell them what to do on set. But Ridley would just smile and say yes to anything. Then go off and shoot what the hell he liked.'

All of which discouraged the so-called fashionable agencies from employing him. The likes of CDP demanded tight control over the way in which their scripts were filmed. Scott preferred to work with larger agencies who would give him creative freedom. 'The people at Young and Rubicam and Ogilvy and Mather allowed me to pursue my own ideas,' he says.

> They weren't perceived in the same way as CDP or DDB creatively but that was good for me because they were willing to let me try new stuff. My commercials were less influenced by clients and executives. I was defying pure advertising logic – the thought that you had to have a very precise, tightly scripted commercial outlining certain things about the product. I was just pursuing scripts that would allow me to make a mini-movie.

Scott became obsessed with breaking into feature films. Having nurtured a cinematic visual style, he knew he had to broaden his repertoire: 'People could see that I could light a beautiful commercial but now I had to prove that I could bring out performances in people. I badly wanted to make ads with dialogue in them to show I was ready to make a film.'

Collett Dickenson Pearce were the experts in such commercials. Their TV campaigns for Nescafé, Birds Eye, Benson and Hedges and Cinzano were renowned for their striking performances, humour and authentic dialogue. But the small agency had its own roster of preferred directors and Ridley Scott's name wasn't on it. 'One day, Colin Millward said to me, "Why don't we ever use Ridley Scott to direct our ads?"' remembers John Salmon. 'I said: "I don't know!" Then we picked up the phone and hired him.' When Scott received the call, he was in Prague filming an SR toothpaste commercial for a rival agency. 'I'd based the whole thing on David Lean's *Dr Zhivago*,' he recalls. 'I was completely running wild with that sort of stuff at the time. But when CDP rang, I realised I'd have to rein myself in a bit.'

His break came with 'Border Crossing', a grandiose commercial for Benson and Hedges which referenced the cold war thrillers of John Le Carré. With its moody, east European location and steam-train setting, it was a script suited entirely to Scott's brand of cinematography. 'Other people who worked at the agency were frightened of the way I worked,' he says. 'But I got on very well with the copywriter, Lindsey Dale, and the ad turned out to be quite beautiful in the end. It was like a very good James Bond film. Even now I will look at it on my historical showreel and can see that it's bloody good.'

Finally, Scott's foot was in the door at CDP. After he impressed Salmon with his heroics on the test shoot for Benson and Hedges' small cigars, the agency offered him a more prestigious project. 'We were working on new ideas to market Hovis bread,' says Salmon.

This was a time when white bread was very popular. But magazine articles had recently been published pointing out that it wasn't particularly healthy. Hovis was only really white bread with some wheatgerm in it. But we thought we could market it as a wholesome alternative. We decided to play on its tradition. It had been manufactured in the same way since the nineteenth century.

A press campaign was devised under the slogan 'Your Daily Bread'. Soon, copywriter Geoffrey Seymour wrote a television script rich in period atmosphere.

The idea didn't fit the usual CDP template; there was no humour or dialogue. Rather, it was a thematic script that described a nostalgic vignette of post-war, working-class life in northern England. As a young boy and his mother walked up a steep cobbled street before a misty sunset, a voice-over rich in northern vowels reminisced about his childhood: 'We walked down to the shops, Mam and me,' he said. 'Just after the war and it was real butter for tea . . .' The ad closed on the slogan: 'Hovis . . . It's as good for you today as it's always been'. For once, CDP didn't need someone to deliver a verbatim interpretation of their script; they needed someone who could generate an atmospheric and visually rich commercial. 'We wanted it to look like an old sepia photograph that had been hand tinted,' says Salmon. 'It was a difficult brief but we thought Ridley would have an idea how to achieve it.'

Having grown up in the North during the post-war period, Scott grasped the theme instantly. The script was a gift to a director with his aesthetic inclinations. 'He was outstanding at composing the frame,' says Salmon, who watched the director spend hours peering through his camera at the softly lit cobbled streets. 'He would art-direct it like a stills photographer. He combined his skills as a trained artist with the instincts he picked up in TV to make a commercial that looked incredible but told a compelling little story too.'

To emphasise the period atmosphere, CDP decided to add a traditional-sounding, brass-band soundtrack. 'The ad manager at Hovis was a sweet old man, but strange,' says John Salmon.

> His attitude was that the ads were something to amuse the salesmen who he employed to drive the bread around to the shops in vans. This was before the supermarkets got a stranglehold on the retail. He said that the ads needed to be changed a couple of times a year to keep the van men happy.
>
> We had already experimented with using brass-band music on a Birds Eye test commercial that was never broadcast. We decided to reuse the idea for Hovis and planned to choose a different song for each subsequent ad in the campaign. But when we put Dvořák's *New World* symphony on Ridley's commercial it sounded perfect. Frank Lowe suggested that we should do what we'd already done with Hamlet and make the music a trademark of the campaign. It had advantages over using a trademark character. Actors are expensive, they grow old and there's always the danger that they could turn into child molesters.

The distinctive soundtrack and deft visuals of the Hovis commercial became a staple of the ad break for two decades. Scott continued to work on the campaign for a period but soon rival directors were aping his revolutionary style. Other stars were emerging in the industry who were bringing their own innovative directing techniques to the ad break. Scott was no longer the only specialist ad director in town. Rather than worry about his reputation, Scott was concerned that his earnings could drop. 'I was a serious businessman by then,' he says. 'I looked around at the other directors who were busy and thought to myself, I should get them working for me.'

Scott asked his friend Graham Terry for advice. 'I told him: "Of course you should start your own production company,"' says Terry. 'Everyone was using Ridley at the time so I knew he'd make a fortune. In fact, I asked if I could come and work for him. But he said: "I'd be mad to employ my best client!"' The director set up Ridley Scott Associates and quickly signed every up-and-coming director he could lay his hands on. 'In a good year I was shooting one hundred and twenty ads. I'd receive my directing fees for each of them plus the commission that went to my company. I could turn them around quickly. It took me a day or two to shoot one and I had it edited by the end of the week,' Scott enthuses. 'But on top of that, my company was making money out of all the other best directors in town. Within a year we were turning over millions.' It was unusual for a creative figure to be so hard headed in business. But Ridley Scott was unusual in many ways. 'Once the company was established I would see him on set shooting an award-winning commercial while signing off company cheques by his camera,' remembers Terry. 'He didn't let a single penny pass through the company without his say-so. That's not the behaviour of a creative maverick. It's the behaviour of a business-man.'

8

'You Can't Scrub
Your Lungs Clean'

By the start of the 1970s, the standard of advertising in Britain had improved dramatically. And the men responsible were starting to feel rather pleased with themselves. 'We used to have a joke in the business about a husband sitting watching TV while his wife was in the kitchen making tea,' says one of them. 'He'd call out to her, "Hurry up, love, the ads are starting!"'

People were talking about the ad break. Businesses ploughed ever more cash into their agencies. And the young men who were now in charge saw their salaries rise ever higher. Many ad executives would swan into work at half-ten in the morning, dash off a couple of thirty-second scripts then disappear for a six-hour lunch. Advertising was riding on the crest of a wave – but for some it wasn't enough. These were individuals who had rebelled against advertising's complacent and wealthy old guard and weren't about to let themselves fall into the same state of bloated mediocrity. Slowly, they began to believe that their creative talents had outgrown advertising. They supposed that their skills could be successfully applied to any medium they chose. And so, with the same sense of pioneering endeavour and supreme confidence that had elevated them to the top of advertising in the first place, they decided to launch an assault on the wider realms of British culture. A few of them succeeded.

One day in the late sixties, Alan Parker got a call from his old colleague Charles Saatchi inviting him to lunch with David Puttnam. The three men met at the Kebab and Houmus restaurant on Charlotte Street and Parker sensed an immediate atmosphere of melodrama. 'Charles leaned across the table and whispered to me, "Alan, we're going to change your life!"' he remembers. Parker gazed back at the two men before him with a mixture of indifference and amusement. 'Go on, tell him, Puttnam,' enthused Saatchi. Puttnam, the bearded, softly spoken deal-broker, glanced shiftily over both shoulders before leaning in and announcing: 'We're going into the film business, Alan. You're going to write the script and I'm going to produce it.' Parker suddenly became more animated. 'Film?' he said. 'Yes.' Puttnam smiled. 'Today is your lucky day. You don't know it yet but we're going to discover you.' Parker, one of the most renowned advertising creatives of his time, took a few moments to consume this, then asked: 'Why are you discovering me? Why can't I discover you?'

They were an improbable trio. Puttnam was a charming, eloquent man about town who had taken advertising by storm with his uncanny salesmanship abilities. When he wasn't working, he was frequenting fashionable nightclubs such as the Ad Lib in the company of star photographers like Terence Donovan, David Bailey and Brian Duffy. Alan Parker was from a working-class quarter of Islington in North London. His appearance may have been rough round the edges but he was a studious worker who eschewed the glamorous antics of his fellow admen. Saatchi was the middle-class son of Iraqi immigrants who lived with his parents in Hampstead.

While flashy in dress and renowned for his expensive taste in sports cars, he was a quiet and intense individual. What little he did say tended to be of a hostile nature. The one trait that all three of them shared was ambition.

Charles Saatchi had drifted silently into Collett Dickenson Pearce. He had left school at seventeen with little idea of what he wanted to do. But time spent working in America had opened his eyes to the fresh, funny and honest advertising being pioneered by Bill Bernbach and his creed. On his return to London, he found work as a junior copywriter at the American-owned agency Benton and Bowles, where he was teamed up with a young art director, John Hegerty.

> One day the boss came in and said, 'I found a writer for you to work with – young guy just starting out in the business' [remembers Hegerty]. I said, 'What's his name?' and he said, 'Charles Saatchi.' I thought to myself: Oh God, he's probably this Italian bloke who lives at home with Mama and can't spell. As it turned out I was right about two out of the three things. He couldn't spell, he lived at home with his mum but he wasn't Italian.

The pair struck up an immediate friendship but struggled to produce work of any note together. Soon, the agency decided to pair the clearly gifted Saatchi with a more experienced art director with whom he would strike up a career-making partnership. Ross Cramer was already renowned in advertising. Tall, good-looking and funny, he was a popular figure who had worked in a number of London's top agencies. 'I moved jobs about once a year,' he says. 'I was determined to avoid feeling like I worked for anyone.' A loud character, he had made waves wherever he'd worked. During a spell at McCann-Erickson, he had learned under the tutorship of the drug-addicted Robert Brownjohn. 'He was incredibly talented and I was in awe of him,' he remembers. 'I used to go and pick him up at his house in the morning and wait outside for ages because he wouldn't get out of bed.' The eccentric American designer would exploit his young apprentice's devotion to the limit. Often, he would offer to cut him in on assorted freelance assignments, asking Cramer to turn his rough sketches into proper layouts. 'We did this pitch for Pirelli and he said if we won the job he'd give me half the money,' says Cramer. 'I worked really hard on it but he came in one day and said, "Sorry, kid, we didn't win the job." I wrote the whole thing off until I found out from someone else that we actually had won the job but Brownjohn had kept all the money for himself. Bear in mind he was on three times my salary at the time.' There was only so much the fiery young art director could take from his mentor. 'I confronted him with it and he just said, "So what? What are you gonna do about it? Hit me?" So I did. I punched him a few times in the head. And he cried.'

Cramer's experience helped bring out the best in Saatchi's writing but Benton and Bowles was a conservative agency in which innovative work was hard to produce. Eventually, they were offered a way out by the agency's former creative chief, Bob Brooks. 'I'd known Bob for a while and he'd offered me jobs in the past which I had refused,' says Cramer.

> He'd set himself up as a photographer and came into see us at our offices in Knightsbridge one day. I remember there was paint dripping from the ceiling all over our work and we were completely miserable. Bob just said casually, 'Why don't you go to CDP?' I told him we didn't know how we could get in there so he went and made a call to Colin Millward. Within half an hour we were asked in for an interview.

Millward was immediately impressed by Cramer's work and gregarious personality. He offered the art director a job on the spot but was less keen on Saatchi. 'Charles was inexperienced and I did all the presenting,' says Cramer. 'He was this enigmatic, silent figure in the background who had very little to do with anyone. If you're like that, people don't tend to like you. Plus, he had this wild curly hair and they just didn't like the look of him.'

Nonetheless, Cramer insisted his young sidekick come with him. Millward reluctantly complied. Once he had his foot in the door, Saatchi made an immediate impression with their early work for Selfridges department store. 'A warning to the under-12's,' read a headline that sat on one of Cramer's strikingly stark white layouts. 'Be on your guard when your parents volunteer a trip to Selfridges Toy Dept. It could be a bribe to get you inside our barber shop,' the text continued. In spite of his aloof persona, Saatchi was able to write with genuine warmth.

David Puttnam was the young account executive charged with selling Cramer and Saatchi's selection of ideas to the clients at Selfridges. 'We had fourteen different ideas to try and get past them,' says Cramer. 'Nobody thought we could do it. Then David came back from the meeting beaming with pride, saying, "I sold thirteen of your ads!" He was on top of the world. Still, Charlie and I called him every cunt under the sun for not selling the fourteenth and sent him back there!'

Puttnam astonished his employers with his deal-making abilities. 'Puttnam was the most incredible wriggler of all time,' says one ex-colleague. 'He could wriggle his way into anything.' Another ex-colleague explains: 'David would simply refuse to leave a room until he got what he wanted.' He not only sold ideas to clients but convinced the media to run adverts in ways that had never been seen before. He booked a six-page fold-out advertisement in *Vogue*. 'I had to actually go down to the printers myself to convince them it was possible to make such a thing because they'd never done it before,' he says. 'I was doing these more and more extravagant things.' His audacity was appreciated by the CDP hierarchy, who lavished him with money. 'The *Guardian* did a report on people's wages, which was the first time anyone started to talk about how much people earned,' he recalls. 'I was twenty-five and earning about £3,300 per year. Judging by the report, I worked out that I was the best-paid person in my age group in the whole country!'

Saatchi and Cramer weren't far behind. They had received a flurry of pay rises in their first year at the agency and, as his confidence grew, Saatchi had emerged as something of a dandy. Cramer took him to a fashionable tailor where he bought a number of flamboyant, three-piece suits that matched Cramer's and the pair took to sporting watch-chains. Saatchi let his black, curly hair grow out into an enormous wiry mass and drove wildly expensive cars including an E-type Jag and a Lincoln Continental. 'When I first met Charles he was very insecure,' says Puttnam.

> He came on holiday with me and my wife a couple of times and he was always very nervous. He was a person still finding himself at that point. But he always had that extravagance. He bought an E-type when he was still living at home with his parents. And I remember he would go out at the weekend and buy six albums at a time, listen to them all at once, then throw five of them in the rubbish if he hadn't instantly taken to them. He would walk out of movies unless they grabbed him right away. He was very creatively restless.

After writing a series of successful ads for Ford, Saatchi was invited as part of a CDP delegation to the car manufacturer's headquarters in Essex. When he sauntered through the door, resplendent in Carnaby Street suit and bird's-nest hair, the strait-laced company chairman was astonished. 'How did he get here?' he asked a colleague, staring in amazement at the scruffy stranger. 'In his Ferrari, I believe,' came the reply.

Cramer and Saatchi's stock continued to rise. When Cramer was called away to a photo-shoot in New York, Saatchi saw an opportunity to strengthen their positions further. 'He went to the bosses telling them that I was taking our portfolio to the New York agencies and they all wanted to hire us,' says Cramer.

He completely made it up but the bosses believed him. The first I heard of it was when I got back and Charlie called me. He asked, 'Would you like shares in CDP?' I said, 'Of course.' He said, 'What about a car? And your salary doubled? Because that's what I've just got you!'[1]

Their employers would do seemingly anything to keep the team happy. 'I remember John Pearce approaching me one day in the corridor and handing me a brown envelope stuffed with cash,' says Cramer. 'He just said, "We're very happy with what you're doing here. Keep it up."'

It seems absurd that anyone would leave such circumstances behind. But soon each of the young executives was heading for the door. One day, Puttnam called in sick to company director Ronnie Dickenson. 'There was something in the tone of his voice I didn't like,' says Puttnam. 'I got the sense he thought I was faking it. That was the last straw and something snapped. My love for them had always been unconditional and at that moment I realised their love for me was conditional.' Puttnam took offence and resigned. Cramer and Saatchi did the same when their ex-colleague, John Hegarty, attracted them to a rival agency called John Collings and Partners. 'We both had an aversion to staying in one place too long,' says Cramer. 'But it was Charles who made me realise that you could live on your wits and never have to work for anyone. If it hadn't been for him I might have stayed at CDP for ever for the security. In the end, he encouraged me to move simply for the sake of moving.'

Just along the corridor from Cramer and Saatchi's office on the fourth floor of CDP's building sat the agency's other star creative team: Alan Parker and Paul Windsor. Windsor was a senior art director who had teamed up with the inexperienced Parker during a brief

[1] Charles Saatchi declined to be interviewed and has not confirmed or denied any of the anecdotes in this book.

spell at Papert Koenig and Lois. When CDP tried to poach Windsor, he insisted that his young copywriter came with him. Reluctantly, Colin Millward agreed to take on Parker. Just like Saatchi, he had crept into CDP by the back door but would make an immediate impact. Having left school at eighteen, he found a job in the post room of a small agency called Maxwell Clark, where he struck up a friendship with a young copywriter called Gray Jolliffe. 'He encouraged me to start writing ads in my spare time,' says Parker. 'I'd write stuff in the evenings and he and the agency copy chief would give each of them marks out of ten. They'd give them back to me with notes on them like "must try harder". It was an amazing apprenticeship.' Parker was the quintessential new adman: he possessed none of the middle-class manners that had informed the formal advertising of old. He was completely unencumbered by any sense of advertising's rules and principles and developed a style of writing that was entirely naturalistic. He demonstrated this in an early press ad for Harvey's Bristol Cream. 'Of late a few people have been looking at their regular glass of Bristol Cream in a new light,' read the text. 'They've been taking to a largish glass not normally reserved for our sherry. Plonking in two or three chunks of ice . . .' And so it went on in its distinctively informal tone. For the first time, imperfect English was used in an advertisement. In tone and language it read more like a trendy magazine editorial than an advertisement for an upscale brand. Parker's method was to write exactly as he spoke. Creative chief Colin Millward took immediate notice: 'He said, "We've spent years putting this product on a pedestal and you've come along and started selling it off a barrow!"' recalls Parker.

Parker soon established himself as one of the agency's stars but, unlike many of his colleagues, he was not interested in the glamorous trappings of success. 'I wasn't Jack the lad out nightclubbing every night, quite the opposite,' he says.

There were a few of us on that fourth floor who had married young and just wanted to get home to the wife and kids at the end of the day. It depends on what your aspirations are: I had to stop telling my dad how much I earned in the end because it was embarrassing really. Years later I was asked in an interview by French journalists what my dad did for a living and I said, 'He's a painter.' They said, 'How marvellous! What style does he paint in?' I said that he only ever painted in one colour so they said, 'Great! Avant-garde!' I said, 'No, he paints railings for the electricity board.'

When the agency offered their star creatives company cars, Parker rejected a flashy sports car in favour of a sensible estate in which to ferry his children. But despite his seemingly dour nature, Parker's work became renowned for its humour. In a poster for the sport Ford GT, he wrote the headline 'Would you let your daughter marry a Ford owner?' beneath a spectacular picture of a bright red sports car illegally parked on the kerb. The text outlined some details of the engine capacity before continuing: 'Boot space: laughable. Petrol consumption: wicked. If you're a bit worried about your future son-in-law just ponder over the trade in value: 5 Escorts plus 3 Cortina Estates plus a Corsair 2000. You could become the first nine car family in your road.' When Parker's comic efforts helped win CDP the Ford account, Colin Millward doubled his salary.

Soon, Parker had been made the head of his own creative group within the agency. Saatchi and Cramer were head of another and Millward encouraged a friendly competitiveness between the two. 'We would call up Alan's extension and put on a voice. We'd pretend to be from another agency and offer him a job,' recalls Cramer. 'I remember sticking a sign up in the corridor where Charles and Ross's section finished and mine began,' recalls Parker. 'It said "Creative Department Starts Here".'

Parker's flair for conversational writing attracted him to television commercials. The early success of campaigns for Hamlet and Benson and Hedges encouraged greater demand among CDP's clients for TV work. Parker himself wrote some early instalments of the famous Hamlet series but soon became frustrated. He realised that serious commercial makers were hard to find among Britain's film-making community. In response, he decided to take matters into his own hands. He asked Colin Millward: 'Can we have some money to experiment in the basement making commercials?' Keen to keep his star writer happy, Millward agreed.

Parker and his colleagues set about turning the dingy, unoccupied basement of CDP's Howland Street offices into a mini-studio: they bought a 16mm camera, some editing equipment and a few lights. Paul Windsor would light the sets, the agency projectionist would operate the camera and Alan Marshall, a member of the TV department, would edit the films. By virtue of having no practical film-making skills, Parker took it upon himself to say 'Action' and 'Cut'. 'At first, we would just make test commercials for clients,' says Parker. 'It was a great way to get new business because we were able to actually show finished work to prospective clients without spending a ton. But then we started to get more and more elaborate.' Parker would often draft in half the company's staff to serve as actors in his test ads.

> John Pearce was showing a client around the office one day and it was completely empty. He was a bit embarrassed and asked a secretary where the hell everyone was and she said, 'They're all in the basement making a commercial with Alan.' I remember the ad: it was supposed to be a huge, pre-revolutionary Russian ball so I got everyone dressed up for it. This client kept seeing women walk across the scruffy hallways in ball gowns and tiaras!

None of Parker's test films was ever broadcast. To his frustration, those that proved popular with clients had to be remade by union-registered directors. Meanwhile, CDP's management became in-creasingly concerned about their top writer wasting time making non-broadcast ads in the basement. Eventually, they came up with a solution: they asked Parker to leave. 'I couldn't believe it when Colin [Millward] and John [Pearce] told me,' he says. 'I'd never been sacked before.' But Millward and Pearce had bigger plans for their protégé: they would underwrite a bank loan to get him started as a fully fledged commercials director. They promised him a raft of their best scripts to direct and told him to get started right away. Effectively, CDP were inventing their very own, in-house director. Parker was bewildered. 'I truly didn't have any ambitions to be a director of any kind,' he says. 'I really took a great deal of pride in being an advertising person. I loved it and if I had any ambitions at that point it would have been to take over from Colin Millward as creative director when he retired. But suddenly I was a full-time ad director.'

A couple of weeks before Parker's directing career began, he'd received Charles Saatchi's lunch invite to the Kebab and Houmus. In the two years since Puttnam had left CDP he had been cultivating a long-term plan to revolutionise the British film industry. His meeting with Parker and Saatchi was to prove a significant milestone in his quest. 'The British film industry was crap,' he says. 'The stuff they were producing was shit and I knew it. But then I saw *The Graduate* starring Dustin Hoffman and I thought to myself for the first time, I could do that. There was nothing in that film that required budget. It was a makeable film. I knew the talents who I believed could write a film like that and I knew the musicians who could create that kind of score.' Convinced that he could emulate Hollywood-standard movies in the UK, Puttnam devised a long-term strategy to raise the necessary funds. Using his knowledge and contacts in the advertising business, he set up a photographer's agency. 'I used it as my stepping stone,' he explains. 'I knew it was a way of earning quite serious sums of money which I could use to finance myself in films.' After two years in the business, Puttnam was ready to make his first step into movies. By the end of their lunch in Charlotte Street, Puttnam had commissioned both Saatchi and Parker to write screenplays. 'They were both writers I knew and I thought they were both really stylish and interesting,' he says. 'I talked to both of them about

113

movies and knew they both worshipped them. If you had to bet on which one of them would have written a better screenplay, it would have been Charles. But ironically, it was Alan who wrote the better one.' Parker's script, *Melody*, was a tale of schoolyard romance which was eventually turned into the film *SWALK*.

For Saatchi, the experience of being second best was an unusual one. His response was to pour even more effort into conquering the ad industry. Things had been going badly at his new agency. He and Cramer discovered that John Collings and Partners was an inherently conservative agency that was resistant to their fresher brand of advertising. During his time as a rookie writer at Benton and Bowles, Saatchi had quietly endured such a predicament. But by now he was a big name in the business and had developed a temper to match. 'He wasn't big on charm,' surmises Cramer. 'He couldn't manage what he said.' The two endured a succession of client meetings in which their ideas were often treated with scepticism and derision. In the end, it got too much for Saatchi. 'Charles rarely opened his mouth in meetings, but when he did, he was so belligerent,' says Cramer.

> In the end, he went mad in the middle of a meeting with a pyjama manufacturer. He was just frustrated that we'd chosen such a bad agency. We had a row about his behaviour and he ended up saying, 'Well, what shall we do?' I said, 'We've just won more awards than anyone else in the business so let's do some consultancy work.'

In the early seventies, there was a huge appetite among clients for modern, CDP-style advertising – but very few individuals who were thought capable of producing it. In such a climate, Saatchi and Cramer were a finite and valuable commodity. 'We looked in [the industry magazine] *Campaign* and found out which agencies were pitching for business,' says Cramer. 'Then we called up and said, "You'll never win that business without us. Pay us a sum and we'll create a pitch for you. If you win it, we want a percentage." '

The strategy proved successful. They set up a company under the banner Cramer Saatchi and began to hire extra staff to deal with the influx of work. John Hegerty followed them from John Collings and the team moved into new offices on the corner of Goodge Street and Tottenham Court Road. By coincidence, the newly renovated building became a hotbed of the industry's leading talent. 'It was a great place to be at that time,' says Hegerty. 'David Puttnam's photographic agency was on the first floor. Boase Massimi Pollitt had just started up on the floor above us and right at the top were the designers Lou Klein and Michael Peters. It felt like a creative hub.'

Martin Boase, the managing director of a fledgling BMP, remembers the separate companies sharing their workload. 'I would bump into Ross and Charlie in the lift and give them some of our briefs to work on when the workload was getting too much,' he says. 'On the day we hired Ernest Marples and got it announced on the ticker in Piccadilly Circus, I bumped into Charles on the stairs. He said, "What a coup!" I always liked to think that we taught him an early lesson about PR.'

Downstairs, Alan Parker and David Puttnam were cultivating their film careers. The occupants of the Goodge Street office block were going 'multimedia' several decades before the term became popularised. 'At that time, we didn't think we should be limited to ads,' says Hegerty. 'We thought we should be making movies and developing programming and stuff like that. It was really way ahead of itself in that sense. All of us in that building had a sense that it was them versus us.'

But it was a straightforward advertising brief that gave Cramer Saatchi their greatest breakthrough. Ross Cramer met a fellow parent at his daughter's school who worked for the Health Education Authority. A conversation at the school gates led to Cramer Saatchi taking on their advertising account. It was hardly the most lucrative piece of business: the organisation needed a small number of posters and brochures produced. But the consultancy realised that the nature of the work – warning the public about everyday health risks such as smoking and food hygiene – had huge creative potential. They eschewed the drab, prosaic literature that the HEA had previously produced in favour of explosive shock tactics. An early anti-smoking poster showed a nicotine-stained hand being scrubbed with a nail brush under the headline 'You Can't Scrub Your Lungs Clean'. A food hygiene poster had even greater impact. Above an appetising image of a steak dinner, the bold text read: 'This is what happens when a fly lands on your food. Flies can't eat solid food, so to soften it up they vomit on it. Then they stamp the vomit in until it's liquid, usually stamping in a few germs for good measure . . .' The revolting description continued before concluding: 'and then, when they've finished eating, it's your turn'. The end line warned: 'Cover food. Cover eating and drinking utensils. Cover dustbins.' Cramer Saatchi had managed to sensationalise dull subjects that, in the early seventies, were not high on the public's agenda. Their blunt, shocking tone caused a stir among the advertising industry too, winning them a slew of D&AD awards.

More was to come. Jeremy Sinclair, a raw trainee recruited straight from Watford Art College, devised a poster aimed at encouraging men to take more responsibility for contraception. The image depicted a sorry-looking man in his twenties sporting a pregnant bulge beneath his V-neck jumper. 'Would you be more careful if it was you that got pregnant?' asked the headline. It sparked an immediate tide of controversy with *Campaign* magazine reporting that many believed it to be 'overstepping the boundaries of good taste'. It became one of the most iconic images of 1970s advertising despite being initially rejected. 'We picked the pregnant man out of Jeremy Sinclair's bins,' recalls Cramer. 'We used to go through everyone's bins at night because we often found that the stuff they threw away was better than the stuff they showed us.'

When the *Sun* newspaper ran a feature article on the men behind these shocking new health warnings, Charles Saatchi began to ponder the importance of PR. Soon, he would use the notoriety of Sinclair's poster as a launch pad for his next venture. He decided that Cramer Saatchi should reform themselves into a fully fledged agency who worked directly for clients. Realising that they would need someone with more business acumen than his current collection of creatives, he approached his younger brother Maurice. Maurice Saatchi had been a star student at the London School of Economics who had gone on to prove a success at Haymarket Publishing, the small magazine company owned by the Conservative MP Michael Heseltine. Aged twenty-four, Maurice was a star executive, driving to work in a 1966 Corvette and, just like his brother, adorning himself in expensive suits. The pair seemed to share a natural flair for attention-grabbing behaviour, although Maurice was the more contemplative of the two.

Charles decided that his brother could serve as the respectable face of the new agency – which he proposed they call Saatchi Cramer Saatchi. But his old partner had other ideas. Cramer's experiences in the eclectic environs of Goodge Street had given him a taste for other creative pursuits. 'I'd seen Puttnam and Parker getting involved in production and I thought I could do the same,' he says.

> There was an atmosphere at that time in which you felt you could do anything. People were deciding overnight that they were going to switch from writing ads to being photographers – even if they'd never held a camera before. And they were succeeding too! I decided that I wanted to direct. I didn't know much about film but I knew that I at least had the personality to get actors to do what I wanted.

Working in another small agency didn't appeal to Cramer. Plus, his relationship with Saatchi was deteriorating. 'We were in a meeting with the people from the Health Education Authority, one of whom was called Lady Burke,' says Cramer. 'She was in charge of the HEA

117

magazine and politely suggested that the poster we'd made didn't require a full point at the end of the headline. Charles snapped at her and shouted, "Listen, Lady Burke, don't tell me where to put my full point or I'll tell you where to put your magazine!"' As he grew more successful, Saatchi seemed to grow more aggressive. 'He wanted everything his own way and would go mad if he didn't get it,' says Cramer. 'He became obsessive about tiny things like cars arriving on time. He didn't have much compassion with the people around him, which is fine when you're a kid but when you're older and the boss it becomes too much. People were scared of him. We started to row: I took to slamming a steel ruler down by his hand to scare him.'

Cramer had met Maurice when he'd popped into their offices on occasion and found him to be 'clearly extremely brilliant'. But he was reluctant to join him in business. 'I didn't want to be a book between Charles and Maurice,' he says. 'I could smell where it was all going and I thought they would eat me alive.' When he left to become a director, the two brothers changed the name of the new agency to Saatchi and Saatchi. John Ritchie, Charles's former CDP colleague, advised the young executive: 'You're mad to try this out. You should stick to what you know.' Saatchi replied: 'I can't turn back now. I've got my brother involved.' Ritchie promised him that, if the agency failed, he would always be welcome back at CDP. But Saatchi was increasingly consumed by what Puttnam describes as an 'overwhelming ambition'. Increasingly, creative concerns gave way to a more crude desire for mass accumulation. Towards the end of their relationship, Cramer and Saatchi went out on a shopping trip together to buy a wedding present for a mutual friend. Cramer led them to a gallery where they pondered the purchase of a small Miró etching. 'There were two to choose from and I said to Charlie, "Which one do you prefer?"' recalls Cramer. 'He just glanced at them and said, "Let's get the one with the biggest signature."'

118

9

'I Put My Brutus Jeans On'

In the mid-1970s, British advertising was booming – and ad directors were the new kings of the industry. 'We were a group of people living in a bubble,' explains one leading director of the time.

> We thought we were celebrities. Of course, no one knew who the fuck we were in the real world. But if we walked down the street in Soho everyone recognised us because they worked in the same industry. So we convinced ourselves that we were famous. When we flew, we'd fly first class and sit in the departure lounge, dressed from head to toe in designer gear, next to a rock star and a Hollywood actress. It probably wasn't a very healthy state of mind for some of us.

In the early years of advertising's creative revolution, copywriters and art directors had been the pioneers. But a decade on, the industry placed all of its emphasis on TV commercials and the technical maestros who made them. 'For the moment British advertising seems to have hit a plateau creatively,' wrote Bob Brooks in the 1974 D&AD annual. 'Technically there is hardly a bad-looking television commercial around'. Lighting, direction and casting are for the most part excellent but in general new ideas do not seem to be getting through.' Hugh Hudson agreed: '1973 was bankrupt in ideas and produced a marked lack of advertising originality. The profession conveniently hides behind technique.' Both men had sat as judges at that year's awards – and both felt that directors were the only people keeping adland's credibility alive. Both men were themselves ad directors. Not that they were entirely blinkered to the talents of others: 'The only relief during two days' viewing,' Hudson had concluded in his D&AD entry, 'was the outstanding directorial ability of Alan Parker.'

Parker's directing career began in spectacular fashion. He appeared to take to the new film-making discipline with ease, directing award-winning commercials at a prolific rate. Fuelled by an influx of scripts from his patrons at CDP, the fledgling director applied the same homely tone to his commercials as he had done as a writer. His commercials for some of the biggest consumer brands in the country were infused with a style and humour that were distinctively British. In 1974 alone, he produced award-winning ads for John Smith's, Nescafé, Cockburns and Birds Eye. He specialised in tiny vignettes depicting everyday life in Britain. They were rich in quirky dialogue, regional accents and oddball characterisation. Football fans who refused to leave Yorkshire for fear of missing their local beer; couples who slumped in front of the TV arguing about instant coffee; scruff-bag kids who liked to make pictures out of their frozen burgers: all human life was there. He tapped into the awkwardness of the British class system: his Cockburns commercial saw a mismatched social gathering aboard a rescue boat after a shipwreck. While the steering-class passengers struggled to correctly pronounce the name of the sherry, the officers patronisingly chuckled and wondered whether anyone had managed to save the petits fours. 'Before Parker, people in TV ads were plastic wrapped, neither old nor young, and never went to the lavatory,' John Webster later surmised. 'Alan changed all that with a whole parade of characters who had creases in their shirts, blew their noses and talked like the milkman.'

Parker's watchword was realism. 'I was the first to go and cast a commercial outside of London,' he says.

> Ads had only ever featured middle-class English accents because all businesses were based in London. Advertising and business people couldn't imagine that people didn't speak the same way as they did. It was a leftover from the class system that a posh accent carries more authority. That's why it was always posh people reading the news. Advertisers used the same theory: if you showed posh people having After Eights at a dinner party, you'll convince not-so-posh people who'd never had a dinner party in their lives to buy them too. But my heroes at the time were people like Ken Loach who were doing incredibly interesting things in television drama by using real people.

With their kitchen-sink ambience, Parker's warm depictions of domestic lives defined the ad-style of the times. 'We called them 2CK ads,' says Frank Lowe. 'Because they always revolved around Two Cunts in a Kitchen. Or if it was for beer we'd call it a "Three P Ad", meaning three pricks in a pub.' For Parker, it provided an often-unhappy comparison with London's other top director. 'If a script said, "We see a beautiful girl walking along a sun-kissed beach in Barbados" – Ridley Scott did that,' he says. 'And if it said, "We see an overweight family in a Shepherd's Bush kitchen, I did those. I did the funny ones, he did the pretty ones. Ridley didn't know how to shoot sound until five years into his career and that's all I'd ever done. We always did different things."

Scott had been watching Parker's progress with keen interest. 'I thought to myself, If he's going to be that good I might as well get him for my own company,' says Scott. 'It's well known that I started trying to pursue him obsessively.' But the partnership was never likely to materialise. 'By the mid-seventies he was cleaning up at his end and I was cleaning up at mine,' says Parker.

> So we had a couple of lunches to discuss combining our two companies. But I said, 'I'm not going to work for Ridley Scott Associates' and he said, 'Well, I'm not going to work for the Alan Parker Film Company.' We talked about starting a whole new company but couldn't come to an agreement about whether to call the new company Parker Scott or Scott Parker and, after a third lunch discussing this, we realised if we couldn't come to an agreement on that, it was never going to work.

Nonetheless, Scott's company continued to flourish, not least because of the flourishing career of his younger brother, Tony. Like Ridley, Tony Scott had studied at the Royal College of Art but had no ambitions to follow his brother into advertising. 'I'd been at art school for eight years and built up quite a bit of debt with my dad during that time,' he says. 'I had my heart set on going on to make films at the British Film Institute but Ridley said, "Fuck that, come and make ads with me and you can pay Dad off in a year." '

The older Scott was keen for his brother to share in his spiralling success. Initially, Tony would film the close-up 'hand shots' of the products that appeared at the end of Ridley's commercials. Soon, he advanced to making commercials of his own. 'Ridley went out of his way to get Tony the breaks,' remembers Graham Terry, the ad agency producer who had commissioned much of Ridley's early work. 'He told me, "Give the next job to Tony and I promise that I'll reshoot it for nothing if he fucks it up." But Tony turned out to be brilliant too.' With the same artistic education as his older brother, Tony Scott proved similarly adept at making visually rich mini-epics. He took over directing duties on the long-running Hovis campaign his brother had started, producing a series of similarly lavish ads set on the cobbled streets of Northern England. But he soon cultivated his own distinctive style. Between 1976 and 1978, Tony Scott made a series of heavily stylised commercials that marked a striking change of tone in the British commercial break. For Brutus jeans he made a commercial that was the antithesis of Alan Parker's domestic dramas. Beautiful models in tight jeans, heavy make-up and little else danced to a thumping pop music score. It was fast-cut, frantic and free of narrative. Similarly styled commercials followed for Berlei underwear (in which models cavorted in their underwear in a black perspex tunnel brandishing neon lighting strips) and Lee Cooper (in which a blue-jean-clad couple perform a sexually charged dance routine in a busy street). 'While Alan Parker was doing the dialogue-driven ads and Ridley was making the arty ones, I cornered the market in sexy, rock 'n' roll stuff,' says Tony Scott. 'There were so few limitations at the time and the agencies just let me get away with anything.' Fashion brands in particular clamoured for Tony Scott to lend their commercials a touch of this racy new aesthetic.

The younger Scott shared his brother's relentless work ethic. He would shoot constantly, often making two commercials at once. 'He would shoot all day for one agency then drive to another studio to shoot a separate commercial through the night,' says one of his RSA production team. 'Then in the morning he'd go back to the original shoot without any sleep. He had to keep it a secret from the two agencies involved in case they thought they weren't getting his undivided attention.' Any earnest leanings towards serious film-making that he might have harboured soon disappeared once he'd tasted the lucrative and exciting world of adverts. 'From the start I had a blast,' he says. 'I had a run of ten years straight making commercials during which I got the chance to fuck my way around the world. I was paid to film in exotic locations and meet the most beautiful girls I'd ever seen in my life. I couldn't believe it.'

Tony Scott combined the sensibilities of a fine artist with the hedonistic predilections of a rock star. 'Both the Scott brothers were dangerous to be with but Tony was probably the maddest,' says Sid

Roberson. 'He drove a Ferrari but I would refuse to get into it with him. Every journey would be like a high-speed movie chase.' With his taste for fast cars, beautiful blondes and enormous Cuban cigars, Tony Scott embraced the role of superstar director long before he'd made it to Hollywood. 'We were making a car commercial at an airfield and the safety officer told Tony that he wasn't insured to smoke cigars on the tarmac, only on the grass,' says a former producer. 'Tony liked to have a cigar in his mouth pretty much all the time. So he got the prop man to make him a square board covered in grass which he would place under his feet whenever he wanted to light up on the tarmac.'

Also represented by Ridley Scott Associates was Hugh Hudson, the film editor and documentary maker who had successfully turned his hand to commercials. An ex-Etonian, Hudson was considered by the industry to have a sophisticated touch, as demonstrated by a much-admired 1973 commercial for Dubonnet, in which sophisticated Gallic drinkers frolicked in the midday sun. In the early seventies, it was a rare taste of exotic, Continental culture amidst an ad break otherwise crammed with Parker's '2CK' commercials. But Hudson could also turn his hand to comedy, presiding over Birds Eye's long running frozen pie campaign which featured the actress June Whitfield and the slogan 'Birds Eye Pies Make A Dishonest Woman Of You'. As one of the busiest directors of the seventies, he was an obvious target for the entrepreneurial Scott. 'I was producing good work and he saw the possibility of making good money out of me and he did,' says Hudson.

After a while I said to him: 'Look, Ridley, I've been working for you for five years and I've contributed a lot of work and a lot of awards. We're now one of the strongest companies in London and I think I've contributed enough to ask for a piece of your company. And he said 'No' without hesitation. I don't hold it against him. He's a completely unpretentious person, just down to earth. Money is his first driving force, family is his second. He happens to have a brilliant visual eye and he drives it to make money.

One former colleague is more blunt in his assessment of the Scott family's financial sensibilities: 'The joke in the industry was always: "What do you get if you drop a penny between the Scott brothers? A metre of copper wire!"'

The jibes did nothing to dampen Ridley Scott's lust for success. 'Soho in those days was vibrant and exciting,' he says. 'We were busy and wealthy for our age and I was skipping everywhere I went. Great success is a brilliant feeling, I can tell you.'

But Scott was disconcerted by the growing tide of competition. His principal rival was the young producer Jennie Armstrong, who, at the start of the seventies, had broken away from top Soho production company MRM to set up her own business, Jennie and Co. She had grown astonished at the wild extravagances that had started to plague advertising. Ad agencies were paying production companies huge sums to commit their ideas to film. Production companies would charge agencies up to fifty per cent of the production budget as commission for their work and a small group of top directors were able to command extravagant daily fees. Travelling the globe to shoot ever more elaborate commercials, they and their production teams began to lose touch with reality, as Jennie Armstrong witnessed. 'MRM had been shooting a major commercial for an oil company in locations across Europe but the whole thing had gone disastrously over budget and over deadline,' she says.

I was called in to take over as producer and couldn't believe what was happening. Someone had bought a Rolls-Royce to use as a camera car! The first thing I did was sell it. The director was furious because he'd assumed that he would get to keep it once the shoot was over. That's the way things worked back then. Directors would always try to cast actors who were the same size as them. That way, they could get the wardrobe department to kit them out

125

in Armani suits which the director would keep once the shoot was finished.

Armstrong resolved to form a smaller, leaner and more austere production company. 'I despised the decadence and kickbacks that seemed to be the rule of thumb when it came to working with certain big agencies,' she says. She left MRM, taking three members of staff with her. One of them was a young producer who she intended to launch as a director. His name was Adrian Lyne.

Lyne had ambled his way into advertising production via an unlikely stint in accounting. 'I joined an accountancy firm straight from school. I hated it but couldn't work out what else to do,' he says. 'Then, a man who worked at my company told me, "If you really don't know what you want to do you should go into advertising and that will help you decide because you can try out all sorts of different jobs within an agency."' After a spell in the post room at J Walter Thompson, Lyne began working for a number of production companies in Soho, finally ending up at MRM. "I was this sort of half-arsed producer," he explains.

> I had my own desk and we would fly all over the world to shoot ads in the most exotic places. But I wasn't very good at it. The drawers to my desk would always have receipts and foreign currency spilling out of them. I was completely disorganised. But there was this fabulous atmosphere about Soho at that time so I just loved working there.

Soon, he began to develop his own creative aspirations. 'I became fascinated by people like Jean-Luc Godard and Ingmar Bergman,' he says.

> It was a very exciting period in cinema. I would go to the Everyman Cinema in Hampstead where they would show all the latest European films. I remember waiting passionately for the

next Truffaut to come out. Watching the way these films were put together made me think about directing. I remember the very moment it happened: I was watching this tracking shot that Godard did of someone walking down the road. The figure was sort of bottom right and most of the frame was just a huge wall. It was a really interesting shot. I thought to myself, I want to do that. I want to make that choice – make the decisions that would get people to notice things.

His first opportunity came at MRM, where he was asked to make a short introductory sequence for their showreel. 'The only brief was that it had to include the sentence "This demonstration film is produced by MRM Productions",' he says. 'Instead of just having this written across a blank screen, I got some rubber stamps made up and stamped the words across a woman's body. It wasn't that saucy, just a nice little idea. And it meant I had my first tiny bit of film.'

It was enough to convince Jennie Armstrong that Lyne had potential as a director. But convincing others of his talent proved difficult. 'It was horrendous,' he says. 'For my first three years as a director I did virtually no work. I had been earning five thousand pounds a year as a producer, which was quite a lot. Suddenly, that fell to two thousand a year and I had three kids to support so it was a tough time. But I never dreamt of quitting.'

Armstrong stood by the aspiring director – but her fledgling company was in need of more work: 'I never lost faith in Adrian, but it was clear that, in order for the company to survive, I'd have to take on a director who worked more regularly,' she says. That director was Alan Parker. 'Colin Millward was a confidant of mine at the time and I told him that I was looking for a director who could help make a success of the company,' she recalls. 'Colin put me together with Alan, who agreed to work with me if I personally produced his work and gave him independence from the company to do what he liked.'

Parker's rampant success was enough to help Jennie and Co. flourish while Lyne struggled to get his directing career started. 'I had a room in Jennie's office in Beak Street and as I rushed in every day I would pass Adrian's little office,' recalls Parker. 'I would stick my head in the door and ask, "Any work today, then?" and he'd always say, "Nah." I'd tell him, "Never mind, maybe next week." But it seemed to go on for ever.' Lyne found it hard to witness the success of his colleague. 'Mostly, I was seething with jealousy towards Alan,' he confesses. 'He would work every week and I would have to watch him running in and out of the office, frantically busy while I just sat there in my room, cutting pictures out of magazines and sticking them on the wall for inspiration. I spent a lot of time learning to type just for something to do.'

Eventually, Armstrong helped Lyne make a short film he had written called *The Table*. 'It was based loosely on what my wife and I were going through at the time,' he says. 'It centred on a man accusing his wife of infidelity over the breakfast table. I tried to tell the whole thing without showing too much of the people – just their eyes and body language. People talked about it and we ended up getting it shown on the telly.'

The film helped Lyne develop a reputation for clever visual styling. Soon, even Parker was enviously eyeing his work. 'After he made that film it was clear he had artistic talent,' says Armstrong. 'I think Alan was just as jealous of Adrian as Adrian was of him. Alan might have been busier but all of his work tended to be dialogue driven. He would have liked to do more visual stuff and he could see that Adrian had a wonderful artistic eye.'

Eventually, Lyne received a break: he was hired to direct a commercial for Midnight Mint chocolates. 'It was a set at a party in a small country house with a night exterior. And the whole thing had to be shot in one day,' he recalls.

I didn't have the slightest idea what I was doing. I spent the whole morning trying to set up this incredibly complex reflected shot in the mirror in a bid to make it interesting. I got hopelessly fucking muddled and ended up shooting nothing for the whole morning. By lunchtime, I was sitting in the lavatory crying.

Having stuck by him for three years, Armstrong was stunned by his mental collapse. 'He emerged from the toilet and said, "I don't think directing is for me,"' she remembers. 'The client and the people from the agency were panic stricken. It was the low point of both his and my career.' Lyne was adamant that he couldn't continue.

I told Jennie straight: 'I cannot stand this, I don't want to do this any more. Nothing is worth this nightmare.' I said I'd carry on until seven p.m. when we had to be out of the house. For the rest of the afternoon, because I had mentally dismissed the idea of actually finishing this ad, the pressure was off. I did the rest of the shoot in an almost ecstatic state. It was extraordinary, as if I'd become a different person. Suddenly, everything started working.

Lyne's career gradually began to take off. Soon, Armstrong had two successful directors on her roster, with two opposing work ethics. 'I was used to Alan delivering well-made ads on time and on budget,' she says. 'He had worked in advertising for years and was familiar with the whole thirty-second format. Whereas Adrian was more of an artist whose only considerations were achieving perfection in the lighting and colours. He had no commercial considerations whatsoever.' Lyne confirms. 'I couldn't have given a fuck about selling things,' he says. 'I was never by any stretch of the imagination an adman. I could not stand advertising. All I wanted to do was make films.'

All of which rendered him something of a liability for agencies. 'I went out to America to shoot a commercial for Levi's on Route 66,' he recalls. 'The men from the agency didn't seem used to the way I was working and they went berserk at me. The thing was, I loathed the whole formal process of shooting a film. All that loading the clapper and shouting "Action". I just wanted to get as much stuff on camera as I could.' Lyne ran roughshod over the agency's carefully written script, shunning the precise shot list and storyboards in favour of capturing spontaneous shots of his surroundings. 'I was trying to make a pastiche of American culture: capturing the Greyhound bus, the crop-dusting plane and the cop cars,' he says. 'But it drove the clients and the agency men nuts. The copywriter went mad at me and I walked off into the middle of the desert. I felt sorry for him in a way – knowing that he had to go back to his agency with all these seemingly disconnected shots that were supposed to be a jeans advert.' Once agency and director had settled their differences, the ad was completed and eventually won a D&AD award for out-standing film photography.

Lyne developed a reputation as a maverick in every sense. Blessed with good looks and charm, he was renowned as the industry's most prolific womaniser. 'I remember visiting the offices of Jennie and Co. in the mid-seventies and seeing a beautiful young PA jerking her head out of the fourth-floor window,' says a leading creative director of the time. 'When I got inside I realised Adrian had been inside having sex with her from behind. This was in broad daylight. He was quite insatiable.' In the period following the breakdown of his first marriage, Lyne cultivated a raging bachelor lifestyle. He moved in with two recently divorced friends: a copywriter from CDP called Jeff Seymour and a director called David Ashwell. 'For six months I was carefree,' recalls Lyne. 'We all enjoyed being single. One of my housemates, I won't say which, had an iron bed in the room next door to mine. When I didn't have a woman back myself I would listen to them at it next door.'

His housemates were useful in other ways too: Jeff Seymour soon secured Lyne the job of directing a CDP commercial for the newly launched Ford Capri. 'Jeffery had written it and suggested Adrian to film it,' recalls John Salmon, the agency's creative director. 'I was aware of Adrian's working methods so I only gave him a loose brief. I said, "Just make sure you get a front three-quarter shot of the car because that's what Ford want."'' But even this simple instruction proved beyond the lawless instincts of Lyne.

> They came back after a very long time shooting in Spain with absolutely reams and reams of film. I looked at it all and said, 'Very nice but where's the front three-quarter shot of the car?' Adrian said: 'Oh, we didn't shoot that, it's a bloody cliché!' I said: 'Well, yes, it is a cliché. But as I told you, Ford won't pay us unless we give them that shot. And if Ford don't pay us, we won't pay you. So you'd better go and get one for us!'

It took another two reshoots before Lyne finally deigned to produce the desired shot. 'I didn't really want to show close-ups of the fucking car,' the director says. 'It was a nice ad – like a little love story really. It had impact in itself but they kept insisting on this bloody shot so in the end I gave it to them.'

Despite his unpredictable behaviour, the industry's most successful agencies continued to gamble on Lyne. 'Adrian was more difficult to work with than any of the other top directors because of his lifestyle,' says John Webster, creative director of Boase Massimi Pollitt during the same period.

> Sometimes, he didn't turn up on time at the shoot. And you could never tell what he was going to do before he did it. All you could do was give him a vague idea of the brief and then just hope he produced something close. I remember once on set he started shouting: 'Get me a wheelchair!' He'd got it into his head he needed to be wheeled around at high speed. So we all watched his assistant rush him around in this wheelchair while he filmed everything with a hand-held camera.

Perhaps the most successful expression of Lyne's unconventional style was his 1976 commercial for Brutus jeans. The shoot had been orchestrated amidst a familiar air of pandemonium. 'There were male and female dancers in the script but by six o'clock in the evening I hadn't done a single shot of the men!' he laughs. 'The client from Brutus was there on the set and he freaked out. He got up and said, "Right, that's it, I'm taking the account away from you!" And stormed off. I was saying to the people from the agency: "Who's going to pay now? Shall I carry on or what?" In the end I decided to finish it regardless and managed to get everything filmed by eleven o'clock that night.' The results were striking. In similarity to his Levi's advert, it shunned narrative in favour of high-impact, heavily stylised imagery and a blaring soundtrack. It adhered to neither the hard-sell advertising of old or the more subtle, comedy-driven ads of the late sixties and seventies. Instead, it sought to generate a sense of 'cool' around the product. 'They sold so many pairs of jeans that they had to stop putting the ad out because they'd run out of product!' claims Lyne. 'I know that is true.'

Not only was it a precursor to many of the ads that were to follow in the 1980s, it provided a template for the burgeoning revolution in music videos that would take off with the launch of MTV in 1981. Indeed, the song that Lyne had commissioned as the advert's soundtrack – 'Jeans On' by David Dundas – became a top ten hit in the UK charts. Again, the advert's impact on the music scene was the first hint of a trend that would explode during the following decade. 'His quick cutting style and way of shooting women in this sexual manner was revolutionary at the time,' says fellow director Bob Brooks. 'Brutus was the first commercial that overtly used sex as a selling device. All of his commercials were more erotic than anything that had been seen before.'

Lyne's emergence coincided with that of Tony Scott and only intensified the competitive atmosphere among Soho's directing elite. 'Adrian and I were always in competition for the same scripts because both of us were using that MTV style before MTV even existed,' says Tony Scott. 'We would all try to get hold of each other's showreels so we could study what everyone else was doing. I would steal ideas sometimes and still do. I'm the world's greatest

132

plagiarist. Why not?' Lyne relished the rivalries. 'I was told that when Ridley saw a commercial I'd made for Black Magic he was so impressed that his heart sank,' he says. 'I was very flattered by that.' Jennie Armstrong remembers:

> There were huge egos at play among the directors at that time. There would be such a fuss if one director stole someone else's cameraman! My offices were just round the corner from Ridley's in Soho and we all used to bump into each other in the local restaurants. It was quite amicable on the surface but people used to joke that one day Ridley would emerge from underneath one of the tablecloths with a machine gun to wipe the rest of us out!

Ridley Scott was determined to be the first of Soho's ad makers to graduate to Hollywood. 'In the mid-seventies we were really hot and I started to think, How am I going to get to make a film?' he says.

> I wrote three screenplays myself before I ever got lucky. One of them came close to actually being released. It was with the Bee Gees, whose career was struggling at the time. It was the year in which *Tommy* had been a success for the Who so they wanted to try something similar. It was a medieval film starring them but, unfortunately, they refused to actually sing in it. And I had a hunch that people wanted to see the Bee Gees sing, not act. In the end the whole thing collapsed due to financial problems. I honestly thought the film thing was never going to happen at one stage.

Meanwhile, Alan Parker was quietly pursuing his own film career. In 1971 David Puttnam had successfully produced his first screenplay, *Melody.* 'I had no concerted plan to get into films at that stage,' says Parker. 'I ended up getting into them due to David Puttnam's ambition.' Puttnam hired TV director Waris Hussein to direct the film but Parker was an influential figure on set. 'One day we were shooting this huge sequence on a school playing field and we weren't doing very well,' says Puttnam. 'I asked Alan if he would go off and direct some extra footage. He came back flushed with excitement at the end of the day and said, "That's it! That's what I want to do!" Without doubt, by the end of that day, he wanted to be a film director.'

Parker self-financed a fifty-minute film called *No Hard Feelings*, which he sold to the BBC. Its success led to an approach from the broadcaster's drama department, which asked him to direct a Jack Rosenthal script called *The Evacuees*. The wartime story of two Jewish boys evacuated from Manchester to Blackpool played to all the strengths Parker had harnessed in advertising and, in 1976, the play won him a Bafta. 'It proved I could do something longer and therefore made me an easier sell for Puttnam,' he says.

Directing children had become Parker's forte. In a bid to exploit this talent on a grander scale, he wrote a feature-length screenplay called *Bugsy Malone*. Based on a Depression-era gangster film, all the parts were played by children who used cream-squirting 'splurge guns' rather than real bullets. Puttnam doggedly pursued finance (although Parker would again plough some personal funding into the project) and the film went into production in 1975. 'I was sick when I found out that Parker had got a film,' remembers Ridley Scott. 'I didn't sleep for a week.'

It was clear that David Puttnam was becoming the British film industry's kingmaker. 'I don't think either Alan or Ridley would, in an ideal world, have wanted me to be their producer,' he says. 'It's just that both of them couldn't get a film offer.' Parker had tried to develop movie projects first through Jennie and Co., then the Alan Parker Film Company, but to no avail: 'We were considered to be somewhat bubblegum because we'd come from a commercial world and were used to selling things,' he says. Scott's efforts were hindered by similar prejudices. 'When I got to Hollywood it was hard to make people take my advertising work seriously,' he says.

I would take my reel to a movie executive or producer and it was filled with ads that even now, with all my movie experience, I know were pretty formidable. But I'd sit in a darkened room with them playing on screen and the guy would be half looking at them at best. I knew they were good, plus I was financially independent by then. Frankly, some of these movie guys, I wouldn't have even hired the bastards – and here they were ignoring my work! So I'd get up, turn on the lights and say, 'Look, you're obviously busy, I'll come back another day when you've got more time to properly look at this.'

Eventually, Scott realised that Puttnam might be his only hope.
'The breakthrough came when I took *Bugsy Malone* to the Cannes Film Festival in 1976,' says Puttnam.

I had to fight tooth and nail to get it entered because it was a kids' film. But I managed to get it in through a loophole in the rules. That year there was mayhem – every film shown had been more violent than the last one. It was the year of *Taxi Driver* with Robert de Niro. We were the second-to-last film just before closing and the audience – who had been watching nothing but blood and guts for the past two weeks – went berserk! Alan was literally carried out of the cinema shoulder high.

Immediately, Hollywood executives were flocking around Puttnam.

A friend of mine from Paramount Pictures said, 'Have you got anyone else like Parker?' I said, 'I think I might have' and went straight to the phone box. I called Ridley in London and said, 'Get yourself on the first plane over here.' We all had lunch on the beach the following day. Ridley and I had two scripts and wanted to pitch the bigger of the two, which was about the Gunpowder Plot. The guy from Paramount said, 'What's that gonna cost?' and we said about 2.2 million dollars – which was a lot for a film in those days. So he said: 'Oh shit! What about the other one?' I said, 'It's called *The Duellists* and we can make it for 1.4 million.' He said: 'Fine. I'll take that one.'

The Duellists, a grand military drama set in the Napoleonic era, was released the following year, winning Scott a best first work award at the Cannes Film Festival. Finally, both Parker and Scott had a foothold in the film business. But the stigma of their advertising backgrounds wouldn't go away. 'I became extremely sensitive about the way in which our advertising backgrounds were perceived,' says Parker.

> I remember reviews that said things like 'Alan Parker comes from the world of advertising which gives us an easy stick to beat him with'. I was affected by that sort of thing and that was why I eventually stopped making ads altogether. Ridley got clobbered for his background even more than me because his work was thought to be so visually slick, like a soap powder commercial. Of course, what the critics didn't realise at the time was that they were looking at the greatest cinematic visual stylist of his age. He didn't care, though. Whenever I got worried about what critics wrote he'd say, 'Oh, fuck 'em – ask them how much they earn!'

Parker immersed himself in a film career that was to make him one of Hollywood's most successful directors over the next decade. Scott experienced similar success but, between blockbuster movies such as *Alien* and *Blade Runner*, continued to make commercials. 'Parker and the others thought their ad career held them back and jeopardised their credibility,' he says.

> And they were right – it was a problem. But I didn't give a shit about the credibility and I didn't give a shit about the word on the street either. I wanted to shoot films whatever they were. The more you shoot the better. You bounce a ball and shoot at the net every day of the week and you've got a better chance of scoring than if you only do it once a week. That was always my attitude and my brother's too. We always supported each other in that.

Ridley Scott Associates continued to flourish even when the two brothers left for Hollywood in the eighties. While there, Tony Scott found himself in competition with Adrian Lyne once again. 'I was offered the chance to make *Flashdance* before Adrian,' he says. 'I turned it down but Adrian took it on because his daughter had started to watch MTV. I think he looked at the script and said, "I'm gonna do one and a half hours of MTV with this piece of shit!" ' The result, a superficial but stylish tale of a Pittsburgh steel worker who dreams of joining ballet school, was the catalyst for Lyne's long-running movie career. Tony Scott's early films included blockbusters such as *Top Gun* and *Beverly Hills Cop II*. They exemplified what ad directors initially brought to features. Rich with blaring, pop-rock soundtracks, stunning visuals and fast-paced editing, his style would define the 1980s genre of blockbuster popularised by the Hollywood producers who became his patrons: Don Simpson and Jerry Bruckheimer. 'Jerry [Bruckheimer] was the first person to see the energy and dynamism that ad directors could bring to movies because he was from a commercials background himself,' says Tony Scott. 'I never turned my back on making commercials, though. Making a movie takes a piece of your soul. Making ads is more fun.'

Arguably, British advertising had been influencing film-makers long before the likes of Scott and Parker arrived in Hollywood. The vast resources and freedom made available to ad directors during advertising's boom era of the seventies enabled them to innovate and experiment with new techniques that weren't possible in TV or film. The lavish production values applied to commercials during that period were already being noticed by leading Hollywood figures. As Adrian Lyne recalls:

I remember making this ad up in Yorkshire when I got a message that Stanley Kubrick had called. He'd seen an ad I'd made for milk in which I'd used a particular type of graduated filter. He wanted to know exactly which filter I'd used. I rang him back from a phone box, my hand shaking. He ended up offering me the role of second unit director on *Barry Lyndon*. I should have done it but I didn't. I thought that if I'd done a good job he'd get the credit and if I did a bad job, I'd get the blame.

Tony Scott was similarly surprised to discover a fascination with commercials among Hollywood's elite.

I made a telecom commercial in Italy with Marlon Brando and he told me that he wanted to make ads and asked if I would be his commercials agent, he says. 'He was my hero so I said, "Sure." Then he showed me twenty-six scripts he'd written for [the haemorrhoid cream] Preparation H and said, "Do you think you can sell them?" I promised to try but the only interest I got was from *Saturday Night Live*, who wanted to run them as a series of weekly sketches. They liked the idea of introducing an item each week by saying, "And now for Marlon Brando's Preparation H commercials, directed by Tony Scott!" But he died before we ever got it off the ground.

By the early eighties, Hollywood would be awash with the cream of British advertising talent. Adrian Lyne, Alan Parker, Hugh Hudson and the Scott brothers would each use the skills they had honed in commercials to forge successful movie careers. The generation that had sparked adland's creative revolution was now ready to apply their creative talents to a far grander sphere. 'I have never underestimated the part advertising has played in my career,' says Ridley Scott. 'It was my school and my university and it absolutely shaped what I do now.'

10

'Refreshes the Parts Other Beers Cannot Reach'

On his sixtieth birthday, the staff of Collett Dickenson Pearce had presented John Pearce with a rare Chevrolet bull. In the 1970s ad world, carriage clocks, gold watches or cigarette cases just wouldn't do. Pearce kept the animal on the grounds of his vast country home, along with the rest of his collection of rare cattle. Advertising, and his agency in particular, was embarking upon an exuberant period of decadence in which the whimsical purchase of novelty bloodstock seemed perfectly normal. But for Pearce, it would soon come to an end. In 1971, he had a heart attack during a CDP board meeting. He survived but his role at the agency would never be the same again. At around the same time, the agency lost a number of the key creative figures who had helped build its reputation. Some foresaw the end of the line for CDP. But a new management team would soon guide the agency to the most successful period in its history; and make their predecessors seem positively austere in the process.

By the end of the decade, CDP's decadence would come back to haunt the management when they were investigated for tax avoidance – a case that would eventually reach the Old Bailey. 'The Inland Revenue had a list of suspicious things that we'd spent company money on,' says Salmon. 'When John Pearce's Chevrolet bull was brought up, the judge found it hilarious! It actually helped the situation a great deal.' But bloodstock was just part of CDP's catalogue of excesses during the 1970s. As the agency had grown from its ramshackle roots in north Soho, it had embraced its ever-increasing success with both hands. Helicopter rides were not unusual. An agency yacht had been purchased and moored off the south of France. Staff accounts at Savile Row tailors were de rigueur. And American Express cards with limitless expense accounts were standard issue for all members of their creative department. The departure of key staff like Alan Parker, Charles Saatchi and David Puttnam at the start of the seventies had done nothing to knock the agency off its stride. A new generation of creative talent wasn't far behind and, over the course of the decade, they would help build the once small but fashionable company into the leading ad agency in the world, practising an ethic of hedonistic endeavour as they did so.

'I was elected to the board and started to attend meetings,' remembers Salmon.

They would only take about eight minutes and would usually be held in the corridor. At the end, I noticed that someone would walk around with a tray of brown envelopes and everyone would get one. I turned to one of the other guys and said, 'What are they?' He explained they were our 'round sum allowance'. I asked him what that meant and he said, 'Oh, you know, it covers incidental expenses like taking people out to lunch or paying for taxis.' I thought, How very intelligent. It was completely separate to my salary. In fact, at one stage the allowance got so big I barely needed to dip into my salary at all!

While Britain's economy spiralled into inflationary chaos, advertising's own inflation rates ran even higher.

At CDP we were making fifteen per cent mark-up on an inflating budget from clients like Benson and Hedges. Money was raining into the pot. At the same time, the top level of income tax was running at over eighty per cent so it was pointless having a raise because the Revenue took it all. Harold Wilson's government imposed a law saying that companies couldn't distribute profits to their shareholders beyond a certain percentage. The idea was that companies would reinvest money in 'the plant'. But in advertising agencies there wasn't a plant. Just some typewriters. So there was an enormous amount of money just washing around in the agency.

Company management soon discovered imaginative ways of spending the surplus. 'The agency told me that it wasn't worth giving me a pay rise because of the tax situation so they asked me what I'd like instead,' says Salmon. 'I said that I'd always wanted a car with a chauffeur so they gave me a Mercedes 450 SEL and a driver. We also had a company who would buy all of our suits and rent them back to us to save us having to spend our own money on them. It was crazy.'

It may have resembled the last days of the Roman Empire – but there were few signs that these extravagances were undermining CDP's success. Their list of blue-chip clients expanded continuously, as did their yearly haul of awards. This heady era of success was presided over by a new, young management figure whose eccentricities would match those of his predecessors, Pearce and Colin Millward. 'I remember the day that Frank Lowe started at CDP,' says Alan Parker. 'Everyone said, "There's a star account executive

141

joining from Benton and Bowles and you two are just not going to get along.'' He walked into the office dressed head to toe in black to mark the anniversary of Manchester United's Munich air disaster. I realised then he wasn't an ordinary suit.'

Until he joined CDP in the late sixties, Frank Lowe had seen advertising merely as a conduit to a life of glamour in swinging London. 'I grew up above my granny's pub in Manchester called the Wagon and Horses,' he says.

> My mother was an opera singer and my father was in the RAF and neither of them were around much. I got sent away to boarding school at the age of two and a half. I ended up spending most of my adolescence at a school near the Yorkshire Moors, which was all very Dickensian. By the age of seventeen I couldn't take the idea of one more institution so I packed up my bags and decided to start work right away.

He broke into advertising at JWT and then spent a period in the United States before returning to London, where he made a name for himself as an unusually effective account executive. His charm and determination helped him cultivate strong relationships with clients at a succession of agencies – but he harboured little enthusiasm for the ads themselves. 'It was all pretty awful stuff and I had very little interest in advertising at that time,' he says. 'It was just a means of earning good money and meeting girls really.' Lowe moved into a flat off the Cromwell Road in west London with the CDP art director Vernon Howe, where the two enjoyed a carefree bachelor existence. 'We would go Alvaro's restaurant on the King's Road and hang out with Bailey and all the rock musicians every night. Because he was an art director, Vernon knew all the top models who he would bring around. They were wonderful times.'

Eventually, Howe introduced Lowe to more than just beautiful women. 'Vernon said that they were looking for an account person at CDP because they were pitching for Birds Eye and had no one who knew anything about packaged goods. So I went along for an interview with Colin Millward and they offered me the job right away. I asked for five grand. They gave me five and a half plus a Lotus Elan.'

Soon, he discovered his new agency had a distinctive way of working. 'The first thing I had to sell was a Birds Eye frozen pies commercial starring June Whitfield,' he recalls.

> After we made the presentation to the clients, Colin Millward turned to me and said, 'Well, let's see what this hot shot account executive thinks about it.' To my eternal shame I said, 'I think I'd rather have the creative department's view first.' Colin said: 'Well, we don't need you, then, you can fuck off.' I was so upset that I threatened to quit to John Pearce. But he said, 'Take no notice, that's just the way we are at Colletts.' Eventually, I fell in love with the agency.

Lowe revelled in the agency's unforgiving atmosphere and discovered a new passion for his work. 'There was a level of perfectionism that I hadn't seen at any other agency I'd worked at,' he says.

> I learned everything I could from John Pearce. He taught me that, as ad makers, we were going into people's living rooms on the TV every night, that they hadn't invited you in and that we should therefore be courteous to them during our visit, show them a little respect, and avoid shouting at them. He also told me to be honest with clients. Account men have traditionally been regarded as professional liars: people who would say anything to a client just to sell them the work. But at CDP I learned that, if you were presenting work that you really thought was excellent, there was no need to lie to anyone.

Lowe soon discovered his own creative instincts. 'I'd formed friendships with people in the industry who were creatives and thought for a time that I'd be able to do what they did,' he says.

143

But one day I was sitting in a restaurant with David Bailey and I said, 'What is it that makes you able to see and think the way you do?' He said: 'It's quite simple – you need to observe. Do you observe?' I said, 'I don't know.' So he put his hands over my eyes and said, 'We've been sitting in this restaurant for the past forty minutes. Describe every single thing in here to me from the flowers to the tablecloths to the wallpaper.' I couldn't describe a thing. It was a sad lesson for me and I realised I couldn't never be an art director. So I decided that I might as well do whatever I was good at. I decided I wanted to be the very best account man there was. That way, I thought people might respect me in the same way that I respected the best writers or directors. They'd say, 'Frank can't art-direct or use a camera, but, God, he can't half recognise a good idea when he sees one.'

The creative figures at CDP were notoriously hostile to members of their account department. On his first day at the agency, John Salmon had seen one senior account executive flying out of an office in the creative department. 'I was walking along the corridor when this chap in a suit crashed through the door, hit the wall and slumped to the ground. That was the respect with which their opinions were usually treated.' But Frank Lowe began to change this traditional dynamic by showing greater interest in the creative process. 'Far from being in conflict with him, we loved him because he was beautifully encouraging about good creative work and the most brilliant salesman when it came to convincing the client of its value,' says Alan Parker. 'Everyone loved working on his accounts because you automatically produced good work.'

When John Pearce suffered a heart attack during a board meeting in 1971, his place at the agency helm was inherited jointly by Bob Pethick (who had previously served as deputy creative director) and the account executive Geoffrey Pattie. But when Pearce eventually recovered and returned to the agency part time, more radical changes were made. Pattie went on to pursue a political career, which would eventually see him become a cabinet minister under Margaret Thatcher, and Pethick retired. Frank Lowe, still in his thirties, was appointed CDP's managing director.

A new era of expansion and ostentatious success was ushered in by Lowe. He combined everything he had learned from Pearce and Millward with his own natural flamboyance and aggression. The company moved out of their scruffy Howland Street offices and into a smart block on Euston Road. Alan Parker, who had resolved to turn his back on advertising once his film career had taken off, was lured back on an exclusive contract thanks to Lowe's persuasive powers. 'I offered him twenty commercials per year,' he explains.

> But this would mean that he couldn't work for any other agency. I thought he was the best director of dialogue in the world at the time so it was well worth it. And it meant that he could be guaranteed about a hundred grand a year from ads. I went to Malta to finalise the deal while he was finishing *Midnight Express* and [David] Puttnam was furious. But I explained that it would mean he could concentrate on great films and that his wife and kids wouldn't have to worry about money.

John Salmon, who succeeded Colin Millward as creative director during Lowe's era, remembers the grandiose style Lowe brought to the agency: 'He liked helicopters and used them whenever he could,' he says. 'I remember once flying to Brands Hatch with him by helicopter to test-drive the new range of Fiats.' While he was generally popular among his own staff, the wider industry often perceived Lowe as a Machiavellian figure. He was branded manipulative, egotistical and ruthless by rivals; characteristics that were hardly rare elsewhere in the industry. But like all talented self-publicists, Lowe did little to dispel the rumours. Instead, he watched in amusement as myriad apocryphal stories circulated around the industry. One concerned a CDP Christmas party in which Lowe allegedly found himself in a lift with a beautiful young secretary.

145

'Fancy a blowjob, Frank?' the woman is reputed to have asked. 'What's in it for me?' came his response.

Like his predecessors, Lowe tolerated the peculiarities of his creative staff's behaviour. 'My attitude was: anything is excusable if you have talent,' he says. But he was no soft touch. When copywriter Terry Lovelock was briefed to relaunch the Dutch beer brand Heineken, Lowe was displeased with the time it took him to conjure a suitable idea. 'Frank had reduced the whole brief down to one word: "refreshment",' Lovelock remembers. 'I was banging my head against the wall for months trying to think of something and I was getting nowhere. The pressure was increasing so I managed to sneak out of the country on the back of a separate shoot.' Lovelock's creative partner, Vernon Howe, was supervising the production of a Ford commercial in the Moroccan desert. On the flimsy premise that his assistance might be required, Lovelock managed to book himself a company ticket to fly to Marrakesh and avoid the increasingly agitated Lowe. 'He was due in my office with his ideas on the Monday morning but he just didn't turn up,' recalls Lowe. 'I asked the secretary, "Where the hell is Terry?" and she said, "He's going to Marrakesh. He's on the way to the airport right now." So I called him up in the British Airways first-class lounge at Heathrow and said, "I don't know what you think you're doing, Terry, but if you don't come back by next Monday with a line for Heineken, you're fired!"'

Lovelock was frozen. Holed up in a luxury Marrakesh hotel while his colleagues spent long days filming in the desert, he found himself unable to write. 'I drank a lot of beer and went out shopping in the markets, trying to distract myself,' he says.

One night I was deserted by my guide after being conned by a trader in the market. I got completely lost and almost didn't find my way home. After that I was too scared to go out. I stayed out for a second week, by which time I assumed I had lost my job. I just sat around the hotel feeding the local cats sardines. Then one night I woke up with two lines in my head. They were both similar in style:

they were supposed to be a parody of an old-fashioned slogan for toothpaste like: 'Colgate freshens your breath while it cleans your teeth'. One of the lines I wrote was 'Heineken refreshes the parts that other beers can't reach'. But I was sure they'd think the word 'parts' sounded too sexual. Still, at least I had something to go back to Frank with.

Despite his prolonged absence, Lowe felt unable to fire the writer. 'He had talent so I couldn't have sacked him really,' he says.

Terry was a dear sweet boy but as mad as a hatter. He presented me with these lines he'd written on the back of an envelope. I read 'Heineken Refreshes the Parts Other Beers Cannot Reach' and said, 'Terry, that's wonderful!' He seemed quite surprised. It was perfect because Heineken were looking for something which would run for a while and obviously it was a very versatile line.

Lowe instructed Lovelock to write a script, then set about selling the idea to the client.

The following week, Lowe found himself on a plane bound for Moscow with Heineken's head of marketing, Anthony Simonds Gooding. 'What's going on with the Heineken ads?' demanded the client. 'I picked up the sick bag from the seat rack and wrote "Heineken Refreshes the Parts Other Beers Cannot Reach" on it in biro, then handed it to Anthony,' says Lowe. 'It wasn't the most formal of presentations. He looked at it for a while then turned to me and said, "Are you serious?" and I said, "Yes." So he thought about it a bit longer and as we took off he just said, "Well, I'm sure it will be fine."'

Terry Lovelock and Vernon Howe wrote and directed the first TV commercial in the series, in which tired policemen were fed pints of Heineken to revive their aching feet. An early poster demonstrated Heineken's abilities to put Humpty Dumpty back together again. Another showed *Star Trek*'s Dr Spock drinking a pint of Heineken to revive his trademark pointy ears. Lovelock's line formed the basis of a campaign that successfully lasted into the twenty-first century.

With one short line of text, Terry Lovelock had salvaged his CDP career. He soon became a central figure under Frank Lowe's new regime. 'He spent very little time in the agency,' says John Salmon. 'In fact he was always all over the place, but he came up with the Heineken line, which was worth more to us than someone who'd turn up on time every day.' Lovelock's previous career as a jazz musician informed his professional conduct, which consisted largely of long lunches and evenings spent in nightclubs. 'I'd get into the office between ten and eleven,' Lovelock explains. 'Then we'd soon head off to lunch, which was supposed to end at two thirty, but nobody ever did come back. I preferred to work in the restaurant while we ate.' Charlotte Street, just a stone's throw from CDP's offices, had become the capital's restaurant mecca. The Kebab and Houmus and White Tower were two of Britain's first Greek restaurants – and Lovelock and his colleagues proved their most loyal patrons. 'We knew all of the restaurant owners and pub landlords,' he says. 'We'd spend long days in these places coming up with ideas but I would never write drunk. I might come up with ideas after a few drinks but I would wait until the next morning before I actually started writing things up.'

The only figure who came close to matching Lovelock's epicurean reputation was an art director called Alan Waldie. In a characteristically unorthodox management decision, Frank Lowe decided to unite the pair as a creative team. Waldie was a somewhat unusual figure on the London advertising scene: in contrast to the unkempt ragamuffins that dominated the creative scene, he was a dandyish individual with dashing looks and a refined Home Counties accent. He was a graduate of Farnham College in his native Surrey who would develop a twin reputation for artistic flair and enthusiastic hellraising. 'I'd always wanted to be a rock star,' says Waldie. 'And Terry took me to all the places that musicians went. He also introduced me to fine restaurants, fine wines and fine malt whiskies.

We embarked upon a few years of great fun and success together.'
At a young age, Waldie had identified advertising as the perfect
business in which to fulfil his rock-star dreams. 'I wasn't a great
musician but I thought that advertising might be a way of living a
similar lifestyle without actually playing the music,' he says. 'And I
was right.'

His career had started at a small agency called Roger Prior, where
he had immediately experienced the industry's seedier inclinations.
'It became apparent early on that advertising was a strange and
exciting industry to work in,' he says.

> If we got our work done on time the boss would show us a dirty
> book as a reward. One day he showed us something so obscene
> that we took the book and threw it in the Thames in disgust.
> Unfortunately it floated. If he was particularly pleased with what
> we'd done he would take us to the photographic studios we used
> to see a mucky film on the projector. And as an extra-special treat,
> he would occasionally take us to a real-life sex show in Soho.

His reputation for sporadic flashes of artistic brilliance eventually
earned him a job at CDP. 'John Pearce told the others at the agency:
"Give Waldie the brief, let him go off in all directions and scatter his
ideas everywhere because one of them will be of use. The knack is to
spot which one."' Like Lovelock, the agency did little to discourage
Waldie's excesses. 'One day Terry and I were at lunch all afternoon
with about sixteen others from the agency,' he recalls. 'Frank called
up the restaurant and said to the guy on the other end of the line: "I
don't care who's there, just tell them all that they're fired! Except Terry
and Alan, obviously."'

Waldie and Lovelock soon became a well-known double-act
among Soho's drinking fraternity. 'I'd take Waldie to jazz clubs
and he would always end up on stage playing "Mean Woman
Blue" on the piano,' remembers Lovelock. 'I'd play the drums and
people would often think we were a real act.' On the rare occasions

that they were in the office, the couple refused to curtail their excesses. 'There was a period where we had a fridge in our office and that became a great danger,' says Lovelock. 'We ended up using it to create a whole campaign. Other creatives would be lured in by our fully stocked fridge. The deal we offered them was: give us a line for our Walls sausages campaign and you can have a drink from the bar.'

While they shared a taste for alcohol, Waldie's consuming passion was women. 'Terry was less interested in that sort of thing,' he remembers. 'I remember telling him once, "I've got a couple of Negresses lined up for this evening." That was what we called black girls in those days. But Terry was quite prim and proper when it came to women.' Not that it discouraged Waldie. On an early job for CDP, he was sent to Seattle to shoot an Aer Lingus advertisement at the Boeing factory. 'I decided that we needed to get two 747s and fill them both with gorgeous models,' he recalls. 'There were plenty of women in the area who were keen to make a living out of modelling and we hired them all. Of course, they were very accommodating because I was in charge of the shoot. It was a sensational few weeks. I got to the stage where I was thinking, "Why have four women at once when six will do?"'

The sexual revolution was yet to have a significant impact within the walls of Collett Dickenson Pearce, where the atmosphere was heavy with testosterone. 'We would run castings for models in the office,' explains Waldie. 'And someone would say to the girl: "Now look, we think you could be right for this job but first we want to see your legs to make sure." Often, the girl would just say, "Let's cut to the chase," and show us her tits instead!' Most of the women employed at CDP were in lowly assistant positions. 'There was one particular creative who was single and had girlfriends coming out of his ears,' says Waldie. 'I used to hear him every afternoon shouting out to his secretary: "Who am I shagging tonight?"'

His colleagues were persistently astounded by Waldie's behaviour. 'I remember he was at a hotel somewhere on location and he got absolutely plastered,' says John Salmon. 'The manager steered him upstairs to his room and said, "Goodnight, Mr Waldie." Waldie walked straight across the room, opened the window, fell over the balcony, landed on the ground, got up and walked back through the reception, arriving at the bar just as the manager was walking back in having dropped him off upstairs.'

Despite such episodes, Waldie's talent was enough to maintain a privileged status at CDP. When their successful Benson and Hedges campaign needed an overhaul in the late seventies, it was him they turned to. 'Pure Gold From B&H' was a slogan that had featured in numerous iconic advertisements since the sixties. Comedians such as Spike Milligan, Terry Thomas, Eric Sykes and Peter Sellers had starred in adverts directed by the likes of Ridley Scott and Bob Brooks. But as their creative parameters were constantly squeezed by government legislation, a rethink was deemed necessary. 'The government wouldn't ban cigarette ads but they kept restricting what we could and couldn't show in them,' says Lowe.

> We couldn't show blue skies or green grass or people who looked happy or smart. In fact, we couldn't really show people smoking at all because that might imply it was a nice thing to do. In the end, we thought we'd better change the whole campaign. I went to Alan Waldie and said, 'We've got to do something that nobody will understand. Because if they can't understand it, they can't object to it.'

Waldie embraced the brief with characteristic gusto. 'It took us ages to come up with anything,' he recalls. 'I was worried but there was always the Carpenter's Arms round the corner to escape to. We would stand outside in the summer using the wind spoiler of someone's Porsche as a beer tray. That typified our behaviour at that time.' Soon, agency management found a way of containing the errant art director. 'I lived out in Surrey, which was a long way away and I often proved difficult to locate,' he admits.

In the end they realised it would be easier to keep me moving so they got me a car with a transvestite driver called Big Liz. It was Liz's job to keep an eye on me. She'd always arrive in a summer frock and a long wig to pick me up from the pub and make sure I got home. One evening she walked in and said, 'Ready to leave when you are, Mr Waldie,' which was her way of telling me it was time to go. Then this drunk bloke staggered up to her and said, 'You're not a bird! You're a man!' When she denied it, he pulled her wig off. The next thing I knew, Big Liz had head-butted him!

Waldie eventually managed to concoct a new idea for the Benson and Hedges campaign. 'I'd been struggling for months when Frank Lowe stormed into my office and said, "What the bloody hell is going on, Waldie?" ' he says. 'So I presented him with the ideas I'd drawn up and he fell silent for a while.' Waldie presented a series of surrealist images: a mouse hole, a birdcage, some eggshells and a sardine can. The distinctive Benson and Hedges gold box was the only feature that linked the wordless posters. Lowe was aghast. 'I realised that we might have something extraordinary but I couldn't be certain,' he says. 'There had been a Magritte exhibition in town recently that had been popular and I could see its influence. Then again, I hadn't understood his paintings either.' Lowe went in search of a second opinion but found that creative director John Salmon had washed his hands of the project. 'He said, "What on earth are you all doing?" and I told him not to worry,' says Lowe.

But deep down I was agitated about the whole thing. In the end I called Colin Millward, who was by then agency chairman. He was on holiday in Minorca and I asked him if he would come and look at these ads. He flew back to London, came to my house in Chelsea and had dinner. Then, in the morning, I laid all of Waldie's ads out on the floor and asked him what he thought. He stared at them for a few minutes then, with typical ambiguity, said, 'You've got two campaigns here. The surreal one is the good one.' Then he flew back to Minorca.

Assuming he had Millward's approval, Lowe presented the ads to Gallaher, owners of Benson and Hedges. 'I remember showing them to the Chairman of Gallaher, Stuart Moore, with an unusual amount of trepidation,' remembers Lowe. 'And he simply said, "Well, that all sounds very sensible, Frank. Now let's talk about Silk Cut." He showed tremendous courage not only to ditch a previously successful campaign but to replace it with something so radical.'

Waldie commissioned Brian Duffy to photograph the finished advertisements, which were soon plastered across Britain on forty-eight sheet posters. With their surrealist pretensions and total lack of slogan or text, they seemed to represent creative advertising's illogical extremes. The generation who rebelled against literal, hard-sell techniques in the sixties had, by the end of the seventies, dropped every last concession to traditional marketing. Even the product seemed lost amid the distractingly absurd imagery. A British public reared on bold advertising propositions like 'Drinka Pinta Milka Day' stared in bafflement at the B&H posters that emerged on their high streets. But Waldie contended that there was a method to his madness: 'I though the harder to understand they were, the longer people would stand and look at them,' he says. 'Which is the result you want from any ad.' Certainly, the campaign had a widespread impact and the clients were sufficiently pleased with the results to commission a further series of posters.

Meanwhile, the name Alan Waldie had grown in notoriety. The management at Gallaher were pleased with his campaign and demanded an audience with the creative maestro. In advance of the meeting, Waldie was warned that one of the Gallaher party was in possession of an uncommonly large nose — which wasn't a subject for polite conversation. He agreed not to mention the nose as long as the meeting could take place at the Carpenter's Arms. By the time the clients arrived at the pub, Waldie was drunk; he greeted the large-nosed client from across the bar with the words 'Would you like me to scratch the end of your nose? It's much nearer to me than it is to you!' The CDP account executives cringed but Waldie wasn't finished: soon he had swaggered up to the unfortunate client, grabbed him by his protruding facial appendage and said, beaming, 'I'm Alan Waldie, pleased to meet you!' On reflection, Waldie was mildly repentant: 'That's not really the way to treat a client,' he remarks.

Despite such diplomatic disasters, the campaign continued to flourish and soon Benson and Hedges ordered a cinema commercial. 'I decided that the best way to handle a cinema ad was to translate the posters directly on to film,' says Waldie. 'We knew we wanted to start with this image of a swimming pool in the middle of the desert and end with a shot of one of the posters outside Battersea Power Station. Everything we made up in between was hokum pokum.' With nothing in the way of narrative or dialogue, the idea depended entirely on aesthetics; the artistically minded Hugh Hudson was hired to direct. 'Alan Waldie originally presented me little more than this vaguely surreal idea,' says Hudson. 'But I had seen the posters and knew that I could make something very cinematic out of it. Waldie eventually came up with a specific storyboard which I added to. And I decided upon the Arizona desert as the perfect location.'

Frank Lowe took the idea to Gallaher and negotiated a record budget for a commercial. 'The scale of the shoot was immense and the budget worked out to about ten thousand pounds a day – a huge amount back then,' he says. Gallaher were taking a colossal financial gamble on a commercial that had no meaning whatsoever. Before long, their brave investment seemed doomed. 'We'd chosen Arizona partly because we'd been told it never rained there,' says Lowe. 'But on our first morning, it rained so hard that it flooded our bedrooms.' The ad team's arrival had coincided with Arizona's worst period of rain in decades. Trapped as they were in their hotel by the flood, shooting the commercial was out of the question. 'We waited a week for the rain to clear up but it never did,' says Waldie. 'People were starting to say, "Let's pull the plug and go home. We've had enough." But Frank was like a general marshalling his troops. He said: "Bollocks! We've already spent twice the budget. We'll sort this out. Nobody is leaving!"'

Lowe cut an extraordinary figure in their remote desert location. He had taken to carrying a teddy bear under his arm everywhere he went, which he refused to be separated from. 'I think it had something to do with the *Brideshead Revisited* adaptation that was on TV at the time,' says Hudson. A rumour circulated the set that Lowe had missed his original flight to Arizona after realising at check-in that the stuffed toy had not been packed. After returning home in a taxi to fetch the bear, he caught a later flight at great expense. Once in Arizona, he drove about in an enormous hired Cadillac and spent his days calling London to bargain for more money from his clients. 'He should have been dressed as a paratrooper or an American five-star general,' says Waldie. 'It was an enormous crew who needed paying every day even while we weren't shooting,' recalls Hudson. 'We had no insurance but Frank was on the phone to Gallaher every day saying, "We need more money!" It was incredible.' As the budget spiralled beyond £100,000, Gallaher became resigned to the expense. 'In the end they said, "Shut up! Don't call us any more! Just come back with an ad!"' says Lowe. 'And then the rain cleared up.'

Hudson began to assemble the varied facets of Waldie's script: an iguana, a rattlesnake, a swimming pool, a helicopter and a gigantic cigarette box which would be ferried across the desert landscape. The shoot began in earnest. 'One of the iguanas died, tragically,' remembers Lowe.

They had trainers with them and the whole thing was very distressing for everybody. Then Hugh got round to filming the rattlesnake. He put a sheet of glass between his camera and the snake, which allowed him to get the shot where it strikes at the lens. I remember thinking how brave it was for him to lie down there staring it in the face like that. Then the snake handler shouted: 'Hang on, has anyone seen the other rattlesnake?' The stand-in snake had escaped on set. I've never seen a film crew run so fast!

The finished advertisement was epic in scale, lavishly styled and ostensibly devoid of meaning. But it was so striking to cinema audiences across Britain that they applauded whenever it was shown. It was also adored by the advertising industry, which honoured it at the 1980 D&AD ceremony with the coveted (and rarely awarded) gold pencil. That year, the ceremony was held at the Albert Hall and presented by Michael Parkinson, who told Alan Waldie as he arrived onstage to accept his award: 'You might as well stay up here because you've won the next one too!' By the time Waldie had finished collecting his slew of awards for 'Swimming Pool', the audience of industry peers was chanting his name like a football crowd. 'The band 10CC were there that night because they'd made the music for the ad,' recalls Waldie. 'They were one of the biggest bands in the country at the time but they found that night so thrilling that two of them decided to become ad directors afterwards.'

These were remarkable times for television commercials. At the onset of the eighties, the charming, comedic ads that had proved successful during the previous decade were falling out of fashion. The Benson and Hedges 'Swimming Pool' commercial ushered in a new era of grandiose, opulently styled commercials. Shortly after the Arizona shoot was completed, Hudson and Lowe flew to Turin to make an equally spectacular film. The product was the new Fiat Strada; CDP's youngest copywriter, Paul Weiland, had been briefed to make a two-minute commercial to fill the entire break during *News at Ten*. 'I'd seen some footage of the Fiat production line on *Tomorrow's World*,' says Weiland. 'The machines that built the cars looked quite balletic and I thought we could set their movements to classical music. I chose Rossini's *Figaro* – simply because it rhymed with "Ritmo", the original name of the car.'

The team arrived in Turin to shoot at Fiat's car plant, only to find the workers on strike and the factory closed. 'That very week, the Red Brigade had shot and killed the director of marketing on the steps of Fiat HQ,' says Lowe. 'The unions were surrounding the factory and we couldn't get in. We had a whole crew sitting doing nothing in the hotel and it felt like Arizona all over again.' Hudson saw an irony in their predicament: 'We were there to make a commercial with the slogan "Hand Built By Robots",' says the director. 'And the workers were striking in protest against the robots taking their jobs.' But Lowe was in no mood for sympathising with the workforce. 'I said, "What we'll do is fly over the top of the picket line in a helicopter." I had no choice.'

Eventually, the crew managed to get into the factory and start filming the futuristic robots in action. But as the union officials began to realise exactly what the team of Brits was doing, tensions erupted. 'The picket line started to burn tyres outside the factory and it started to feel dangerous,' says Weiland. 'Hugh was filming the machines painting the cars with a hand-held camera. He was under immense pressure because we had to get the shots quickly and get out of there.' Having recently completed his first feature film, *Chariots of Fire*, Hudson felt able to cope with the strain of their predicament. 'I felt comfortable shooting things on that scale and in that environment,' he says. 'But in the end we had to escape through the only available exit that wasn't blocked by burning tyres.'

The resulting film was a resounding success: 'When I presented it to the client a few weeks later in Venice he burst into tears and threw his arms around me,' says Lowe. 'I think it was relief. He'd given me this huge budget and seen the whole thing spiral out of control in Italy but never questioned us.' Lowe spent yet more money on buying an entire two-minute ad break in which to run the commercial: 'It was so long we couldn't afford to show it many times,' he says. 'But there's more benefit in showing a great ad once or twice than banging audiences over the head four hundred times with an ad they hate.' The commercial won a gold pencil at D&AD the following year and the coveted Grand Prix at the Cannes Advertising Festival. Ultimately, however, the Fiat Strada was not a huge success. 'It wasn't a very good car,' reasons Lowe. 'As Bill Bernbach said: "Good advertising can only sell a bad product once."'

Within the space of two months, CDP had produced two of the era's defining commercials. John Webster, the creative director of BMP whose ads were the creative antithesis of such epics, was amazed. 'The swimming pool commercial was one of my favourites of all time,' he says. 'They were really starting to make a whole new style of advertising at that time.' A new epoch of big, bold advertising was heralded. As Margaret Thatcher's Conservative government swept to power in 1979, advertising's new dawn would neatly coincide with the social and political themes of the time. Wealth, ambition and brazen displays of success were simultaneously apparent in the rhetoric of political leaders, the behaviour of ad industry workers and the content of commercials themselves. It was also a new era for Frank Lowe and CDP. In 1981, he would quit the agency and start his own venture – taking much of CDP's creative talent and key clients with him. 'After Frank left people thought things might turn a bit straight,' says John Salmon, who remained as company chairman.

But the madness was embedded. Soon after Frank left we hired a security guard who was always very opulently dressed and would hand out expensive cigars to people as gifts. It was very bizarre and I began to wonder how much we were paying him. It soon transpired that he was renting out our offices to whores from King's Cross after we went home at night. One of our creatives detected semen stains on his sofa and that's how it all came to light. None of this ever seemed particularly unusual.

11

'The World's Favourite Airline'

It was a sunny Saturday afternoon in 1985. Sid Roberson picked up his phone and heard the voice of Charles Saatchi on the other end of the line. 'Time to hit the gentleman's outfitters,' he enthused. Roberson and Saatchi had started out together as lowly juniors in the drab advertising industry of the 1960s. They had both grown up as pioneers of the creative revolution that took place over the next two decades. Now, the two friends were able to enjoy the trappings of their considerable success. 'We would go to Bond Street and spend a fortune on clothes,' recalls Roberson. 'Charlie had a funny way of shopping. If he saw a pair of shoes he liked he would buy several pairs in every single colour. When he saw something he liked he had to own it.'

By the mid-eighties, Roberson was one of London's leading ad directors. Saatchi was a millionaire presiding over the biggest advertising agency in Britain. As they strode out of an expensive boutique weighed down with bags, Saatchi turned to his companion and asked: 'Do you think of yourself as rich?'

'Yes,' said Roberson without hesitation.

'How come?' asked Saatchi, seeming surprised.

'I can buy a new suit, a new car or a new home without having to think twice about it. I don't need to fret about money like most people. That to me is rich,' the director replied.

Saatchi looked back at him incredulously. 'I don't,' he said. 'Until I'm in the Forbes Five Hundred, I consider myself very poor.'

Charles Saatchi never had the same ambitions as his advertising contemporaries. They sought creative credibility, awards, wealth and maybe the odd flashy sports car. But Saatchi wasn't so easily pleased. What he wanted more than anything was world domination. It was an obsession that would make him the most successful British adman of them all. But soon, it would almost destroy him.

Charles Saatchi was driven by a desire to be number one. He was motivated less by a passion for advertising and more by a rampant ambition to succeed by any means necessary. Having discovered an aptitude for writing ads, it became his most viable route to professional success. His brother Maurice watched his early career at CDP with pride: 'I was happy for him because he was doing what he always wanted,' he says. Charles hadn't always wanted to write commercials; he had always wanted to be the best at something. And during his time at CDP in the late sixties, he was considered the best young copywriter in town. After building a successful consultancy with Ross Cramer he quickly set himself a new challenge: to create his own ad agency.

To the small staff of Cramer Saatchi, the transformation into a fully fledged agency seemed like a logical move. They assumed that the new company would seek to establish itself as one of London's 'hot shops': small, fashionable agencies that survived entirely on their creative reputations. But they were wrong. Charles Saatchi was less concerned with the 'craft' of ad making and more with the growth of his business. Making great ads was simply a means to an end.

While his creative ability was considered by many to be second to none, his approach to work was ruthlessly simplistic. In the early days of the agency, a colleague remembers him solving a troublesome campaign for Jaffa oranges by writing copy directly on to an orange, having it photographed and running it as an advertisement. He had little time for advertising's growing air of pretension. When a notoriously precious art director complained that his layouts had been tampered with behind his back, Saatchi was heard to shout at him: 'Who do you think you are? Michael-fucking-angelo?'

The agency he formed in 1970 would reflect these aspects of his personality: it would be creatively ambitious but professionally robust. Received wisdom suggested that the two facets were mutually exclusive, but Saatchi disagreed. During his time at CDP, he had come to believe that the high creative standards they set could be achieved without the fifteen-hour lunches, alcoholic binges and disregard for client relations. He believed that there was a middle way in advertising. And he intended to use it to build the biggest agency in the world.

The agency was built on unusual foundations. After his old partner Ross Cramer had decided to bow out of the venture, Saatchi decided to build the entire company around a small group of creatives. The only businessman brought in to take care of clients, finance and management was a twenty-four-year-old with no experience of advertising whatsoever: his younger brother Maurice.

Maurice Saatchi was born in 1946, three years after Charles. The two had much in common: they were strongly attached to their parents, both remaining in residence at the family home in Hampstead throughout their twenties (well after they had both become millionaires). Maurice was considered the calmer of the pair but his placid exterior belied an ambition to match his brother's. 'I don't really recall having any ambitions as a child,' he says. 'I wanted to do well at school, I suppose, but never thought beyond that. It's hard to say why I developed such a highly ambitious attitude when I started working. These are the mysteries of the universe.'

His first employers were Haymarket Publishing, the magazine company owned by the Conservative MP Michael Heseltine and his partner Lindsay Masters. Maurice's agenda was obvious to both of them. 'He was a young man in a hurry,' says Michael Heseltine.

> When he came for the interview we realised what a sharp bright lad he was and offered him the job on the spot. We told him the pay, which I think was around a thousand pounds a year at the time, and he said, 'No, I can't accept that.' We told him, 'But that's the going rate. That's what people of your sort earn.' He said, 'Maybe other people but I can't live on that.' It was a pretty arrogant tone for such a young man. But we ended up meeting his pay demands. We knew he was a goody – and so he was.

Haymarket had a policy of acquiring failing trade magazines from other publishers and reinventing them. They hired big-name Fleet Street editors and top photographers to reinvigorate previously drab titles such as *Management Today* – and found great success in doing so. Soon after Maurice Saatchi joined, Haymarket acquired an advertising, marketing and PR weekly called *World Press News*. 'It was pathetic,' says Heseltine. 'A real tatty rag. There was no other way to describe it. Small format and drab, faintly creamy paper if I remember rightly. When we turned up at its offices at the Old Bailey to see what we'd just bought I picked up a copy and turned to Lindsay [Masters] and said, *Ad Age*.' *Ad Age* was the weekly bible of the American advertising industry. It covered the comings and goings of Madison Avenue with a relish and style unseen in other industry papers. It was, according to Heseltine, 'the best trade magazine in the world at that time'. He and Masters set themselves the task of turning their newly acquired title into the UK equivalent. A weekly magazine reporting on the increasingly successful, flashy and self-regarding London ad scene was extremely timely. They named it *Campaign*, and their new recruit from LSE became a central figure in its early success. 'At this time I was deeply immersed on the Tory front bench and managing director of Haymarket during a period of immense growth,' says Heseltine. 'I was working round the clock, seven days a week. It was a stretching experience to say the least – I've never been so stressed in my life. Therefore, I wasn't involved in the practical detail of what we did with *Campaign*. I set the strategy and the execution was Lindsay's with a great deal of help from Maurice.' Heseltine's busy schedule favoured Saatchi; he was called upon to take greater responsibility for the new title in his boss's absence and grasped the opportunity with both hands. 'When he was here there was some confusion as to who he worked for – me or Lindsay,' says Heseltine. 'My guess is that he was so omnipresent in my office that people assumed he was my assistant. Then again, he was in and out of everyone's office. The truth was, he was working for himself!'

Saatchi's memories are more humble. 'I was Michael Heseltine's very junior assistant,' he says. 'I remember him saying that the advertising industry was very news oriented, so his idea was to have a newspaper format for what became *Campaign* – with news on the front page. So that's what I helped to develop.' In the space of just two years, he had made a lasting impression on his employers. 'He was energetic and always fun to have around,' says Heseltine. 'But he was very ambitious so we knew he wouldn't be around for long.'

When Charles approached Maurice about partnering him in his new agency, there was some surprise – not least on the part of Maurice himself. While he'd admired his brother's career from a distance, he had never harboured an ambition to enter the industry himself. 'I had never thought about working with Charles before,' he says. 'But I had got interested in advertising during my time at Haymarket. It was a business that struck me as exciting, dynamic and creative.' Some assumed that the older Saatchi hired his younger brother because he wanted a pliable partner. After years spent alongside the bullish Ross Cramer, Maurice seemed the perfect antidote. Others suggested that Maurice's only appeal was that he provided an unusual and intriguing agency name: Saatchi &

Saatchi. But there was far more that the younger brother brought to the business. He helped secure much of the start-up finance, charming the designer Mary Quant and her husband Alexander Plunket Greene into a major investment. His old Haymarket boss Lindsay Masters was sufficiently impressed with his protégé to invest £25,000 in his new venture, while Heseltine was interested too: 'I was attracted by the investment,' he recalls. 'But I had just become a junior minister in the Heath government and thought it was against the rules. As a matter of fact, I was wrong, I'd just misread the rules.'

More importantly than his ability to raise funds was Maurice's understanding of his brother's vision. The idea that an agency could be both creative and big was difficult to grasp for many in the industry. But Maurice was an outsider who shared his brother's belief that anything was possible. While others would have scoffed at Charles's ambition to take on the world's biggest agencies, Maurice backed him unequivocally. 'From the outset, our ambition was to be number one,' he says. 'We could see it was difficult to combine size and creativity but that's what we were determined to do. We just knew where we were going.'

On 11 September 1970, *Campaign* splashed its front page with the headline: 'Saatchi starts agency with £1m'. Below, a paparazzi-style shot of the brothers (Charles resplendent in a snazzy white suit; Maurice the mysterious new face emerging over his shoulder) dominated the cover, alongside a lengthy and favourable story on the new company. In reality, Saatchi & Saatchi's initial accounts added up to far less than a million pounds. But the brothers had resolved to promote their agency with the same boldness as they promoted their client's products: expertly executed public relations coups would become a key facet of their future success.

In the same week that the *Campaign* story ran, Charles took the audacious step of buying a full-page advertisement in the *Sunday Times*, which outlined the new company's mission statement. It ran under the headline 'Why I Think It's Time For A New Kind Of Advertising', was signed by Saatchi & Saatchi copywriter Jeremy

Sinclair (but ghost-written by a trusted journalist) and positioned Saatchi & Saatchi as pioneers of a fresh approach to advertising. It promised a new, more cost-effective way of buying media space in which to run advertisements, the abolition of traditional account executives and an emphasis on salesmanship over indulgent creativity. It cast the agency firmly as industry outsiders. Many of the promises made in the ad were swiftly abandoned once the realties of day-to-day business set in; but it had done enough to draw attention to the new company. They may have given an illusion of supreme confidence but, in reality, they were racked with nerves. 'Our self-promotion was probably considered unusual by the rest of the industry at the time,' says Maurice. 'But the key moment in our first year was when we realised the agency could actually survive.'

The Saatchis employed a contradictory approach to public relations. As individuals, they were at pains to avoid the limelight. Charles never gave interviews to the press and Maurice was only slightly less reluctant. But when it came to the agency as a whole, they possessed a natural showmanship. They were self-confident to the point of being gauche: their humble start-up agency was presented to the outside world as the thriving epicentre of London advertising. They took smart offices on Soho's Golden Square. When a delegation from the sewing machine company Singer visited, to discuss the possibility of hiring the agency, the brothers were concerned that their HQ might look too modest. As a solution, they went out on to the streets and offered passers-by five pounds each to come inside and pose as office workers for the duration of the meeting. Singer were impressed enough to hand the Saatchis their account.

But they wouldn't have to fake success for long. Maurice continued to surprise his new colleagues with his bold approach to business. At the agency's conception, he had drawn up a meticulous five-year plan, which included the possibility of a public flotation. Gradual growth was of no interest to the Saatchis; they were prepared to do anything in order to achieve their objectives rapidly. Maurice used the sales techniques he had picked up at Haymarket to acquire new business for Saatchi & Saatchi. At the time, there was a convention within the advertising industry that agencies wouldn't court their rival's clients. 'Ha!' says Michael Heseltine. 'Maurice would have had no truck with that!' Nor did he. In fact, he couldn't have been any bolder in his salesmanship: he cold-called endless companies explaining that he would like to pitch for their business despite the fact that they already had an agency.

These were the instincts he had absorbed under Heseltine's tutorship. 'The traditional way that magazines sold advertising space at the time was to get on your feet and wander around the agencies all day,' says Heseltine.

> By and large, you could probably do three visits a day. Supposing you were a very good salesman, you might score a thirty-three per cent strike rate per day, which might be enough to earn your keep. But we decided that we wouldn't visit anybody; instead we would make thirty phone calls per day. Now, you certainly wouldn't get a strike rate as good as thirty-three per cent over the phone. But supposing you got ten per cent? That's three new clients per day – which is three times the amount you would have got on your feet.

This system was revolutionary enough in the sales-intensive publishing industry; but in advertising, where clients were usually acquired through social networking and casual encounters, it was considered a vulgar affront to tradition. The Saatchis were only too willing to offend their industry peers: 'We wanted to make a ripple in the pond,' explains Maurice.

The strategy was both shocking and successful. Jaffa and the *Daily Mail* were early account acquisitions; meanwhile the agency continued its high-profile campaign for the Health Education Authority, which had begun at Cramer Saatchi. Their growing reputation among clients was not just down to Maurice's bullish salesmanship. They had hired a charming account executive called Tim Bell, who swiftly became a central figure in the agency's success.

166

Bell had come to the brothers' attention when he featured in a magazine article entitled 'The Young Lions of British Media'. Part of the Saatchi myth is that Bell was approached with the line: 'We hear you're the best media man in town. We want you to come and work for us'. The reality, says Bell, was far less spectacular: 'I think they interviewed about 148 people before me,' he insists.

> They all turned them down for one reason or another but I said 'yes'.
> There were three reasons I joined: firstly, I was flattered to be asked. Secondly, I thought the pregnant man ad for the Health Education Authority was the best press ad I had ever seen. And thirdly, I was bored of being a media executive and they made it clear that they wanted me to be much more than that. I thought it would be very exciting and, basically, I did everything except write copy.

Tall, elegant, well spoken and so charming that colleagues have commented that 'dogs would cross the street to be kicked by him', Tim Bell was the essential antidote to the menagerie of eccentrics assembled by Saatchi & Saatchi. Charles was enigmatic and volatile; Maurice was implausibly young. 'The joke was that we had to have all our meetings after four because that was when Maurice got out of school,' says John Hegerty. In Tim Bell, the agency had a figure of respectability. 'They were Iraqi Jews at a time when there was still quite a lot of anti-Semitism around,' he says.

> They might have chosen me because I had quite a reasonable, posh background. My father was a professional and I had spent most of my youth in Norfolk, which is a fantastically grand county. I might have seemed more palatable to the outside world. But everyone at the agency was engaged in a revolution. We were a collection of young men fighting the establishment.

167

Bell immediately acquired a position at the heart of the agency, wowing colleagues with his uncanny salesmanship abilities. The advertising press referred to him as 'the third brother' and, before long, he became managing director. Some suggested that he was the real driving force behind the agency's success. 'They were wrong,' he contends.

> The truth is that the reason I did all the things I did was because I was the only one who had any knowledge of how an ad agency was run. Charles had only known creative departments and Maurice had only ever been at Haymarket. I brought to them an understanding of how you organise a production department and so on. Inevitably, I became managing director without ever being appointed. I just appointed myself and they never stopped me. So I ran the business but the credit for Saatchi & Saatchi's success was not mine – it was Charlie's. Charlie was the pure energy.

Charles Saatchi drove his young staff with a passion that was almost evangelical. He installed in them a mantra: 'We used to say: It's good to be big. It's better to be good. It's best to be both,' says Jeremy Sinclair. In order to achieve these aims, Saatchi encouraged an uncompromising work ethic. 'Charlie was completely manic,' says John Hegerty. 'At CDP they were writing great ads and then disappearing for a three-hour lunch. If you did that at Saatchis you were thrown out. We worked with a fantastic intensity – he made us realise that we had to work harder than anyone else because we were young and starting out.' Like everyone else, Bell fell under Charles Saatchi's spell. 'His view was that there wasn't any point in doing something unless you had a large impact,' he says. 'From the start the ambition was to be number one, but he showed us that we had to give up everything else in order to achieve that. We'd all sold our cars, we lived in the office, slept in the office, gave up our social life and just drove the business. We wanted to get there very fast.'

The wider advertising world developed a pantomime impression of Charles Saatchi. 'His enigmatic reputation helped our agency's profile a great deal,' insists Maurice. He was never quoted in the press and rarely seen at industry events; fascination in him grew and a myth developed in which Charles Saatchi was two parts Howard Hughes, one part Darth Vader. Those who worked closely with him saw things differently. 'Unlike many creative directors, he had no ego,' says Hegerty.

> If your idea was better than his he'd say so. Because he would think, well, I'll go with whichever idea is more likely to make me successful. To do that, you have to have an absolute dedication to success. He wasn't interested in his name being the one that was always credited. After all, his name was already on the agency door twice. And because of that attitude, he made people better. They genuinely felt that if they had a great idea it would be taken very seriously and sold to the client. He always encouraged us to take our ideas that one stage farther. He made good people great. Or at least good people even better.

But Charles's temper was fearsome. 'Charlie was a man who didn't suffer fools gladly,' says Bell. 'If he was confronted by someone telling him "you can't do that," he became incensed with rage and, in those days, he was capable of being quite physically aggressive.' His worst rages were invariably focused upon his brother. 'There was an incident where he threw a chair at Maurice,' remembers Hegerty. 'Maurice ducked and it missed him. If it had hit him there would have been a serious injury. Charlie's temper was legendary but the good thing was that he never held a grudge. Five minutes later it was gone, he'd say, "Right, I've made my point, let's move on." '

Bell would often find himself caught in the crossfire. 'My office sat between those of Charles and Maurice so I found myself in the middle of the fighting,' he says. 'Once, in a blind rage, Charlie turned to Maurice and said, "I can't believe you came from the same womb as me!" Then he laughed!' By all accounts, they were the sort

169

of manic outbursts only a brother could forgive. 'Freud's Law of Ambivalence applies,' explains Maurice Saatchi. 'You can love and hate the same object at the same time.'

The fallout from such episodes was usually brief, says Bell.

Maurice and I would storm out when he was being so unreasonable, so unforgiving and so demanding. I would head off to Hyde Park Corner and take a long walk to calm down. Maurice would claim he'd gone as far as the Hyde Park Hotel. We'd compete to see who'd gone farthest. The fact was, we were young men finding our way in a complicated world that resented us and that led to frustrations. And Charlie was usually the most frustrated of all. But I don't think anyone was fearful of him. Everyone at the agency wanted to live up to what he wanted and he never let you feel that you had done so. So you were constantly working harder in a bid to win his approval.

Within the first five years, Saatchi & Saatchi developed a reputation that mirrored that of its leader, combining creative excellence with professional aggression. By 1974, they had begun to acquire a number of other companies, including a small property firm and a Manchester advertising agency. Soon, they expanded into larger offices on Lower Regent Street.

Before long, the Saatchis were looking to purchase far bigger agencies than themselves. Maurice sent out standard letters to some of the grandest, most established agencies in the country proposing improbable takeovers. Even CDP was approached at one stage. Invariably, they were dismissed as laughable – but the approaches at least earned Saatchi & Saatchi a reputation for audacity. In 1975, they were approached by the UK's eleventh-biggest agency, Compton UK Partners, with the suggestion of a merger. Compton was part owned by a major US agency and had been established in London for years. They were perceived as dependable and conservative but were looking for some of the creative verve for which the Saatchis were famed. The brothers saw Compton as appealing partners: their clients included the biggest spender on advertising in the UK, Procter & Gamble. It seemed an unlikely pairing, but eventually the brothers sold their agency to Compton in return for thirty-six per cent of the newly merged company. While it appeared that Saatchi & Saatchi was being taken over, it was generally accepted that this was a reverse takeover in which the brothers would ultimately control the new, larger agency. They agreed to move into Compton's offices on Charlotte Street but insisted that they retain their names on the door; the new agency would be called Saatchi & Saatchi Garland Compton. And just to make sure the wider world knew who were the real winners in the deal, Charles utilised his contacts at *Campaign* to assure that the news was reported with the headline 'Saatchi swallows up the Compton Group'. Compton's executives were furious at this version of events. The rest of the industry looked on with complete shock: this five-year-old company started by two twenty-something brothers had become the fifth biggest ad agency in Britain overnight. And it wouldn't end there.

The new agency went from strength to strength. New business flooded in, with IBM, British Rail and British Leyland among notable new accounts. Meanwhile, several of the original staffers had left. Among them was John Hegerty: 'I'd realised that it had begun to be more about being big rather than being the best,' he says. 'There was always that talk about growth and "shall we buy this or that agency?" and I thought, This is all going to get horrible. After I resigned, Charlie didn't talk to me for about four years. That was the one downside of him in a way – he read into things personally. He was a bit paranoid and had this bunker mentality.' Tim Bell saw several others treated with hostility once they chose to leave. 'If you left, you ceased to exist,' he says. 'In fact, you never even existed in the first place. I won't say it was a religion but it was close. People were emotionally committed to the agency as opposed to rationally committed. We were about hearts and minds.'

In 1978, Tim Bell was on holiday in Barbados when he received an unexpected call from Maurice Saatchi. 'We've been approached by the Conservative Party to do their advertising,' he was told. 'Will you handle the account?' Bell was unenthusiastic. 'I told him "no",' he recalls.

> I said I'd worked at Coleman Prentice and Varley when they had handled the Tory advertising during the 1959 and 1964 elections and seen the incredible disruption it had caused. I said, 'This is going to be a nightmare and it will cost us a fortune in lost business because we'll end up neglecting other clients. But I was told, 'Well, we don't care what you think. We've taken it anyway and you're handling it.' So I came back from holiday, met [Conservative Party head of communications] Gordon Reece and the rest is legend.

The Conservative Party had elected Margaret Thatcher its leader in 1975. By 1978, James Callaghan's minority Labour government was clinging to power thanks only to a House of Commons pact with the Liberal Party. With inflation rates spiralling ever higher and Labour seemingly at the mercy of powerful unions, the Saatchis had identified the Conservative Party as a client with huge potential. 'I don't think Charles and Maurice were particularly political,' says Bell.

> They just saw an opportunity to do great work because selling ideas is always going to produce more dramatic work than selling a product. The Labour government was in disarray, Callaghan was a nobody, the country was going to the bottom of all the league tables and so there was every chance of a Conservative victory at the next election. So we were getting on the bandwagon.

The apolitical Saatchis saw Bell as the only man capable of managing the account. 'Most people in the agency were probably Labour voters, although I can't be sure,' he says. 'But I was absolutely the conventional image of a Conservative voter.'

The first work produced for the party was a television broadcast devised by Charles, in which images of everyday Britain were run in reverse. The dramatic sequence was concluded with Michael Heseltine uttering the slogan 'Backwards or forwards, because we can't go on as we are. Don't hope for a better life – vote for one'. At a time when negative campaigning was considered the vulgar preserve of American politics, the Saatchis decided to mercilessly exploit the Labour government's woes. Their next effort was a poster campaign which ran in the summer of 1978, when James Callaghan appeared certain to call a general election. Conceived by Saatchi creative Andrew Rutherford, it depicted a lengthy queue of unemployed workers snaking into an unemployment office beneath the headline 'Labour Isn't Working'. The poster was run at about twenty sites nationwide but its impact was immense. The Labour Party, who still viewed advertising as a suspicious and crass mode of communication, was outraged. Government minister Denis Healey accused the Conservatives of dishonesty and of 'selling politics like soap powder'. The poster had a bluntness to it that was considered inappropriate to the weightier world of politics. But the Saatchis were in no doubt about their strategy. 'Our job was to précis Mrs Thatcher's philosophy and ideas,' says Maurice. 'Like all of advertising, the poster was based on a brutal simplicity of thought. We got to the point with no vagueness or waffle.' In reality, the bulk of their ads focused on criticising the opposition with little reference to philosophy or ideas. The avoidance of complex issues was a lesson learned from commercial advertising – and it proved just as effective in politics.

The controversy surrounding the poster provoked lengthy coverage in the press, earning the ad, the party and the agency far more publicity than any of them could possibly have afforded in the commercial arena. By September, James Callaghan had announced that he wouldn't be calling an election that year. Margaret Thatcher accused him of being 'chicken' about the prospect of defeat. Many believed that it was the infamous poster which had encouraged his delay. In any event, Callaghan's hesitation led his government into the so-called 'winter of discontent' of 1978/79. As unions fell into dispute with the government over capped pay rises, strikes engulfed the country, impacting severely on the day-to-day lives of the populace. Famously, strike action among local authority workers led to rubbish piling up on the streets while, in some parts of the country, dead bodies were said to be left unburied owing to strike action by gravediggers.

By the time Callaghan called an election in May 1979, his government's popularity was at a new low. Ironically, had he called the election a year previously, it would have stood a greater chance of victory. As it transpired, Margaret Thatcher was elected as prime minister with 43.9 per cent of the votes. Lord Thorneycroft, the party treasurer, claimed that the Saatchi poster of the previous year had effectively 'won the election for the Conservatives'. It was the agency's biggest PR coup yet – and one that would pay dividends for years to come. But not everyone agreed with Thorneycroft's analysis. 'They were in the right place at the right time,' says Michael Heseltine of the agency.

What was great about the 'Labour Isn't Working' slogan was that it said what everybody already knew and believed. And it said it brilliantly. But I think the Conservatives would have won either way in 1979. You never know what contributed but you can't escape from the winter of discontent and the spectre of a Labour prime minister brought to his knees as the crucial factors. The Saatchis caught the moment. But governments lose elections before oppositions win them.

Saatchi & Saatchi was now inextricably linked to Margaret Thatcher and the Conservative Party – and not just in a contractual sense. The new prime minister's dogma – rich in enthusiasm for free markets and entrepreneurial spirit – was perfectly embodied by her ad agency. No matter that much of the decade ahead was to be defined by mass unemployment, a volatile economy, war in the Falklands and the outbreak of an Aids epidemic, Thatcher's rhetoric painted a picture of eighties Britain as a place of success, extravagance and uninhibited aspirations. In the Saatchis, she had found admen that could both promote and embody this alternative history. As their names and faces grew ever more familiar in the mainstream media, the British public developed a sense of the quintessential eighties adman. This was based largely on Maurice Saatchi: a merry-looking executive who combined the sartorial leanings of the British gentleman (pinstripe suit and braces) with the flamboyant details of the youthful creative (bow tie and wide-rimmed spectacles). And in line with the Thatcherite ethos of business endeavour, Saatchi & Saatchi continued to expand. They had bought agencies in Scotland and Ireland for over a million pounds in the late seventies and – by the time they had helped Margaret Thatcher win power – they had usurped J Walter Thompson as the largest advertising agency in the UK. 'Margaret Thatcher championed an aggressive and relentless form of conservatism that people could identify with. Saatchi's approach to advertising was similarly ruthless,' says Tim Bell.

Inevitably, there were concerns that the agency's growth had compromised its creative output. 'When they had started out they were great,' says Paul Arden, who would join the agency shortly after the 1979 general election success. 'But after the merger with Garlands they turned very ordinary. Charlie had moved more to the money side. The 1979 [election campaign] stuff was the only thing that had helped keep their creative profile up. I joined as an art director following the first year in which they'd failed to get anything in the [D&AD] book.'

Founding staff member Jeremy Sinclair had assumed Charles Saatchi's role as creative director by this stage and Arden, already a veteran creative director of several smaller agencies, became a leading figure among a new team of creatives. Their first major triumph was a campaign for British Airways, an account the agency won in 1982 after the brothers had met the airline's chairman, John

King. 'He told me they wanted somebody to execute a new advertising strategy for them,' says Maurice Saatchi. 'And uttered the brief: "We're going upmarket." ' The creative strategy was partly informed by Maurice's enthusiasm for the new concept of globalisation. He had recently come across an article in the *Harvard Business Review* by the business professor Theodore Levitt that outlined the new challenges facing large, multinational companies. He suggested that it was a waste of time and money for such companies to tailor their products and services to the tastes of different regions; and proposed that the future of business lay in producing generic brands that could be sold in the exact same form around the world. While Maurice espoused this new theory to his colleagues at the agency, the process of researching the British Airways account was under way. A statistic was unearthed proving that BA ferried more passengers around the world than any other airline and a slogan was born: 'The World's Favourite Airline'. Riddled with bravado and largesse, it was typical of Saatchi & Saatchi.

The first television commercial in the new campaign would set a new standard in grandiose advertising. Originally, senior members of the creative team had worked on an idea that would parody the film *Casablanca*. Meanwhile, junior creatives Rita Dempsey and Phil Mason had developed an idea intended for a secondary, lower-profile campaign called 'Manhattan'. When agency bosses saw the script, they decided to make it their lead commercial. The ad opened on a suburban street in Britain where residents flung open their front doors and stared into the sky. A crackling exchange between two pilots and an air traffic controller was heard above the rumbling of engines and a bright light shone down from what appeared to be a giant saucer. Only this wasn't a spacecraft but the entire island of Manhattan, coming into land on a UK runway. Had director Richard Longcrane not presented it with such aplomb, it might have seemed absurd. In fact, it was breathtaking.

It was a familiar Saatchi technique: they had taken an airline previously renowned for being downmarket and ailing and advertised it in the most extravagant way possible. It was wildly counter-intuitive and insanely bold. Over subsequent years, the campaign would flourish. In 1984, Tony Scott directed an outlandish commercial set on the moon, reminding people that British Airways had 'more people in more places than any other airline'. The following year, Paul Arden created a similarly upscale advertisement for the airline's Super Shuttle service, espousing the 'five-star breakfasts' and VIP service made available to the average businessman. The newly privatised company enjoyed a remarkable upturn in fortunes while Saatchi & Saatchi's ads continued to fuel the perception of eighties Britain as a hotbed of glamorous business executives and slick, global brands.

The brothers, meanwhile, were striving to apply their globalisation theories to the agency itself. 'Once we'd become the number-one agency in Britain, the aim was immediately to become number one in the world,' says Bell. In the early part of the eighties, the Saatchis embarked upon a spree of international acquistions. By 1985, they were acquiring new companies at an average rate of one a month – not all of which were advertising agencies. Media buying firms, PR companies and management consultancies were all brought under the Saatchi & Saatchi umbrella. Increasingly, the agency seemed to be removing itself from the creative ethos on which its initial success had been founded. Tim Bell had seen enough. 'It was beginning to become much more corporate,' he says. 'I felt that it had lost its original simplistic ethos and it was too complicated. I'd been there for fifteen years, raised it to number one and thought, Well, we've done it and it's not much fun clinging on.' The sheer scale of the agency had destroyed the once close relationship he had shared with the Saatchis.

When you're all sitting together in a little office in Golden Square, you're going to be much closer to each other than when you're running fifty-five thousand people around the world, you're in a huge building and they [the brothers] have got corporate lawyers, accountants and advisers all around them. I don't suppose they would ever admit this but I think they weren't very comfortable with the way the business had become. They were talking about having corporate headquarters and doing all those things that actually had nothing to do with what we were all about.

A brief conversation with Charles Saatchi led to Bell's departure from the agency. Preoccupied by their sprawling empire, the Saatchis had allowed relations with the man once referred to as 'the third brother' to sour irreparably. 'I allowed my relationship to deteriorate with Tim because I was dim,' laments Maurice Saatchi.

The expansionism continued unabated. Central to the swath of takeovers was financial director Martin Sorrell, a young business graduate of Cambridge and Harvard who had impressed the brothers so much as an outside adviser during their merger with Compton that they had eventually hired him. His background was in the more sober environs of financial consultancy, but he relished the fast-paced world of advertising. 'I thought it was interesting because you were only ever as good as your last ad,' he says. 'You didn't have to work your way up for twenty or thirty years and be half dead by the time you reached the top. If you could write a good ad like Charles or manage an account as well as Maurice then the business would grow. It was like entertainment or sport in that all that mattered was your ability to do things.' But Sorrell was less impressed by the way in which the industry was organised. 'It was amateur and very artsy-crafty,' he says. 'It had to become more businesslike and I helped Charles bring more discipline to the business.'

Sorrell helped the brothers devise a takeover strategy whereby funds were raised by the issuing of shares on the stock market. Agencies were bought and the existing management was gradually purchased out depending on their performance over a number of years. It proved consistently successful and, in 1985, was responsible for their biggest purchase yet: that of Ted Bates, a Madison Avenue institution and the third-biggest agency in the world. In creative terms, the British advertising industry had overtaken its American counterpart some years earlier. But this was the first attempt by Brits to conquer New York in a business capacity. To the astonishment of the advertising world, Saatchi & Saatchi bought Ted Bates for $450 million. As a result, it became the biggest advertising agency in the world. But its new status came at a price. The American advertising industry resented the extravagant forays the Saatchis had made into their world: the huge salaries that the brothers had lavished on the staff of their new acquisitions drove costs up across the whole industry. Clients began to complain that their once friendly agencies had suddenly become part of a vast, faceless empire. Many of them took their business elsewhere. The huge sums of money being spent by Saatchi & Saatchi alerted many major clients to the wealth of the advertising industry. As a result, they began to squeeze the fifteen per cent rate of commission they had usually paid their agencies. Some smaller agencies couldn't survive the losses.

Meanwhile, back in London, the staff of Saatchi & Saatchi were on top of the world. Since the early part of the decade, the Charlotte Street empire had replaced Collett Dickenson Pearce as the agency at which everyone wanted to work. Despite the corporate machinations at the top, the creative department was still managing to produce more award-winning campaigns than any of its rivals. Saatchi & Saatchi staffers appeared to have more fun too. The austere working practices that the agency had been founded on in the early seventies had, by the eighties, given way to an unashamedly glamorous culture. 'The so-called adman lifestyle of the eighties was very much associated with Saatchi & Saatchi,' says Tim Bell. 'This was partly because we were the only agency people had heard of in the world. But also we had the decadence and the excess and the money and the excitement.'

Tales of legendary excess in Charlotte Street became the stuff of industry legend. When Charles Saatchi grew concerned that their creative reputation was beginning to dip, they poached the copywriter Jeffery Seymour from CDP for an unprecedented £100,000 salary. 'The rest of us envied him at first,' says Paul Arden, who was already one of the agency's senior creative figures. 'But in the end we thanked him because we were soon in the boardroom saying, "If he gets that much I want it too!" Within a year, hundred-grand salaries became the norm!' Prior to his departure, Tim Bell had been central to an expensive recruitment drive. 'Charlie had grasped that if you paid a creative more than anybody else paid a creative, clearly you appeared more committed to creativity to the outside world. He said to me: "We need to revitalise our reputation. Go and find Jeff Seymour and pay him a hundred grand." So I did and the figure became known throughout the industry as a "Seymour".' When star account executive Jennifer Laing left the agency, Bell lured her back to Charlotte Street by buying her a red Ferrari. Even now, he fails to see the extraordinary nature of the gesture: "I bought Jennifer a Ferrari because we wanted her back and she said, "Buy me a Ferrari." So we did.'

Bell afforded himself the same luxuries as his staff.

There are stories about me using a chauffeur-driven car to go from the office to a restaurant a hundred and fifty yards down the road – and they're absolutely true. I did it. Why? Because I'm lazy, that's why. And because, actually, I was normally heading off somewhere else after the lunch and rather than go through the performance of waiting for the car to arrive, I would take it with me in the first place.

By this stage, Saatchi & Saatchi were taking on their rivals at CDP in terms of largesse as well as creativity. 'We all started drinking in the Carpenter's Arms, which was where all the people from Colletts had always drank,' says Bell.

Being a very old-fashioned pub they didn't stock ice. So Frank Lowe and I would compete to see who would bring the most ice with them. I would get my driver to bring around tons of the stuff in my Jaguar. Frank would get his driver to bring it in his pink American Chevrolet. It was stupid. We were like champions fighting on behalf of our agencies.

Arden, who was eventually appointed the agency's creative director, saw the excesses spiral out of control. 'There was a time when I was first in charge of the creative department where the behaviour was too much,' he says. 'Creative people were being judged on the basis of how long they took for lunch. If you were gone for more than four hours, you must have been the most creative person in the agency. It was like Andy Warhol said: "Art is what you can get away with." '

The contradiction between the grim reality of Britain in the eighties and the glitzy world portrayed during the commercial break is easy to understand: while high unemployment, strike action and rioting raged outside the door, the advertising community was ensconced inside a bubble of wealth and indulgence. While the most successful ads of the 1970s had been grounded in a familiar depiction of real lives, those of the eighties depicted the skewed and distorted visions of admen gone mad. 'Advertising at that time was about aspirations,' explains Tim Bell. 'If you looked at the commercials of the time, it appeared that nobody ever wore anything but a smartly pressed suit, no girls were ever ugly and everything was glamorous. But then why should you bore people to death with reality?'

For the Saatchis, reality was becoming stranger than fiction. Not content with being the world's largest advertising company, they were attempting to infiltrate even grander industries. In September 1987, Maurice Saatchi met Kit McMahon, the chairman of Midland Bank, with a view to purchasing the financial institution for somewhere between £3 and £4 billion. The men who had started out making adverts for department stores and citrus fruit now believed they had what it took to revive the fortunes of one of the world's biggest banks. Such was the credibility they had earned in the City of London, they believed they'd be able to raise the necessary funds for the purchase. But Maurice Saatchi's meeting at the bank didn't go according to plan. His speech on the forces of globalisation wasn't enough to impress McMahon, who was sceptical of the adman's financial expertise. 'To say I have regrets about our dealing with Midland is an understatement,' says Maurice. Charles was characteristically cavalier about the affair: 'We got the money and had one meeting with Midland Bank, at which they told us to piss off – and that was it,' he has been quoted as saying.

Shortly afterwards, the brothers made a similarly ill-fated move for the merchant bank Hill Samuel. Their efforts to strike a deal were hamstrung by news of the aborted Midland takeover leaking to the press. The Saatchis were immediately cast as wild megalomaniacs who had foolishly found themselves out of their depth. The advertising industry laughed at their misplaced arrogance while the City lost confidence in a company that appeared to be losing its grip on reality. Their share price dropped and, as a result, they were unable to raise the funds to buy Hill Samuel. It was easy to mock their audacity – but there was some sense to their foray into banking. Marketing was becoming an increasingly important part of the business and the Saatchis had a great deal to offer. Many believed that their failure in the field had more to do with unfair City suspicion of two Jewish admen who weren't part of their 'old school tie' network.

On 19 October 1987, the London stock exchange suffered its Black Monday: the worst twenty-four-hour crash in its entire history. After seventeen years of relentless success, the senior management of the world's biggest advertising company watched as the value of their shares fell by a third in a single day. The champagne was running dry. Effectively, the agency's ability to buy other firms had been neutralised. Issuing shares on the market would no longer raise the sums necessary. In the same month, Maurice Saatchi wrote to Margaret Thatcher resigning the Conservative Party account. He cited a conflict of interests with other accounts. Now their greatest source of invaluable publicity had been lost too. As the eighties progressed, Saatchi & Saatchi's London office managed to at least maintain its creative credibility: campaigns for Silk Cut, Castlemaine XXXX and the launch of the *Independent* newspaper proved successful award-winners. But as a business, it had been humbled. The story of Saatchi & Saatchi had encapsulated the roller-coaster ride of all those involved in advertising's creative revolution. In less than two decades they had gone from frustrated underlings in a tired and lazy industry to wealthy moguls at the top of a thriving business they had completely transformed. But the rapid success had allowed delusions and decadence to set in and, when the wider economy faltered, they paid dearly for their hubris. By 1989, Saatchi & Saatchi had lost their cherished number-one position to their former protégé Martin Sorrell. In 1985, Sorrell had bought a stake in Wire and Plastic Products, a small company that made wire baskets. 'I was forty, had an acute attack of male menopause and wanted to start up on my own,' he explains. The Saatchis had the sense not to cut their ties with the talented Sorrell, having taken a small number of shares in his new company. Employing the same takeover strategies he had used to such good effect at Saatchi & Saatchi, Sorrell bought J Walter Thompson for £330 million in 1987, followed by the Ogilvy Group in 1989 for £560 million. The acquisitions of the Saatchis paled in comparison – and the entire structure of the global advertising industry was changed for ever.

No other individuals involved in advertising during the same era had attempted to change so much so quickly as the Saatchis. By the end of the eighties, their spectacular era of success appeared to be at an end, but their antics and attitude had made a lasting impression on the industry as a whole. 'We were absolutely relentless,' says Tim Bell.

> Everything we did was focused on growth. We had an agency football team with the sole purpose of playing potential clients and getting our hands on their business. If a client asked 'What time is it?' most agencies would answer, 'What time would you like it to be, sir?' But we would say, 'Are you buying or selling?' Working there was upsetting and hurtful and cruel. It was just a fantastic time.

12

'I Heard it Through the Grapevine'

Every year, Dennis Skinner would enliven the state opening of Parliament with his incessant heckling. As the ceremonial official known as Black Rod marched into the House of Commons carrying his sceptre, the Labour MP for Bolsover would demonstrate his disdain for the pomp and circumstance by shouting: 'Bar him!' Once he was heard to yell: 'You're nowt but a midget!' In 1985, he was rather more topical. As the hapless official entered the parliamentary chamber, Skinner's Derbyshire growl rose above the chatter and barked: 'I bet he drinks Carling Black Label!'

John Webster had once noted that the true measure of an ad's success was its ability to pass into the common lexicon. By the mid-eighties, advertising had infiltrated the public consciousness so much that even Dennis Skinner, the sort of socialist politician instinctively opposed to the rampant march of commercial forces, was quoting a popular lager commercial in Parliament. The line was so recognisable to the massed throng of politicians that loud laughter rang around the house.

The 1980s were the era in which advertising moved to the vanguard of British culture and society. The ads had developed a reputation as the most creatively credible in the world. But it wasn't just industry peers who offered recognition; the public at large often seemed enthralled by the ad break. Clothes commercials proved as effective at dictating notions of style as any fashionable magazine; comedy campaigns for bottled lager attracted warmth similar to that generated by the most popular sitcoms; and viewers followed the unfolding plot of an instant coffee campaign with the same suspense as they watched soap operas.

An explosion in media gave advertisers even more places to showcase their work: a second commercial station, Channel 4, was launched in 1982 and, in 1986, the *Independent* newspaper appeared. Throughout the decade, a revolution in publishing saw an avalanche of new magazines creating yet more fertile ground for advertisers. Style titles like *The Face*, home magazines like *World of Interiors* and numerous women's fashion monthlies drove notions of style, image and 'cool' to the forefront of Britain's consumerist culture.

Everything seemed to fall into place for the advertising industry. Politically, Margaret Thatcher endorsed the unbridled forces of commercialism. Advertising, a disreputable and vulgar business in old Britain, was now a celebrated industry that embodied the spirit of the times. Economically, the deregulation of the stock exchange in 1986 allowed agencies to grow at a startling rate and raise huge sums of money through public flotation, copying the template set by the Saatchis. The rise of international brands encouraged agencies to expand into other countries and handle enormous accounts on behalf of the world's biggest conglomerates.

For those who had worked to revolutionise the industry since the sixties, there was a shared sense of 'mission accomplished'. For many, self-indulgence took hold. At a time of great success, wealth and recognition, the industry's natural inclination towards excess was magnified. In 1984, *Campaign* reported that drug use in the advertising industry was spiralling out of control. Cocaine was the substance of choice, changing hands in the mid-1980s at £60 a gram – stories circulated that production companies offered 'cocaine kickbacks' to agencies in return for work. Vast success was fused with a creeping sense that advertising was experiencing its own Last Days of the Roman Empire. But while the megalomania of the Saatchis and the intemperate behaviour of adland yuppies seemed to define the climate, a small group of individuals were managing to keep their heads while all around them went bananas.

The tone of the commercial break seemed to change the moment the seventies ended. The environment of frozen ready meals, instant mashed potato and warm beer gave way to an altogether more glitzy depiction of Britain. The eighties 'dream' was perhaps best encapsulated by a 1988 ad for Volkswagen. Doyle Dane Bernbach's London office produced a commercial starring the model Paula Hamilton as the archetypal Sloane Ranger – complete with Princess Diana hairstyle and shoulder-padded power-suit. Having walked out on her husband, we see her exit a smart mews house and furiously discard her earrings, necklace and fur coat. The one thing she can't throw away is the keys to her Volkswagen Golf, which she climbs into with a defiant smile before speeding away. 'If only everything in life was as reliable as a Volkswagen,' went the slogan. The common touch might have been the secret of great advertising in the sixties and seventies but this was quite the opposite: it portrayed a lifestyle completely alien to the greater part of the country. But with a grocer's daughter running the country, aspiration became a powerful marketing tool. Throughout the decade, the Nescafé Gold Blend campaign presented a mid-market instant coffee brand as the choice of Yuppie Britain. A simmering romance played out between a pair of sophisticated neighbours in a trendy apartment building was enough to keep viewers enthralled over several years – but the campaign was never recognised at industry award ceremonies.

If it wasn't yuppie fantasies in the commercial break it was a new brand of ironic, laddish humour. Ten years before the term 'new lad' was coined in the press, the advertising industry was using the cheeky humour and cultural reference points of the white, working-class male to sell lager to the masses. Dennis Skinner's Carling Black Label allusion came from a long-running campaign devised by Wight Collins Rutherford Scott, an archetypal eighties agency formed by alumni from CDP and Saatchi & Saatchi. In one of the campaign's most popular ads, a stage production of *Hamlet* descends into farce. The lead actor holds the skull of his dead friend and laments 'Alas, poor Yorick . . .' before dropping the skull, catching it on his foot, performing a series of ball skills and kicking it into the lap of a spectator. 'I bet he drinks Carling Black Label,' concludes the skull. BMP's John Webster continued to create enduring comic characters as the ambassadors for mass-market brands: for Hofmeister lager he invented George, a cockney bear lured out of his forest domain to the pubs of London in pursuit of his favourite beer. Meanwhile, a previously unknown Australian comic called Paul Hogan played a confused visitor to London in a series of commercials for Foster's lager. 'Could you tell me the way to Cockfosters?' he is asked by a Japanese tourist on the underground. 'Drink it warm, mate,' replies Hogan, before muttering to himself, 'Funny question.'

Brash advertising reflected a brash culture among much of the industry. But certain agencies tried to buck the trend. Like the rest of his generation of ad makers, David Abbott had grown up in thrall to the work of Bill Bernbach. Unlike his peers, Abbott was able to learn directly from his hero. 'When I ended up running Doyle Dane Bernbach in London, Bill used to come over and I would have lunch with him,' recalls Abbott.

I would invite other people from the office and he would sit there at the table, listening to them talk and answering their questions. I remember thinking, How could any client not buy this man's recommendations? He was very persuasive in a non-manipulative way. He was reserved and had a huge bag of evidence to prove what he did and said was right. You felt you were in the presence of a professional, not some salesman. He dressed discreetly, like a banker. He was a grown-up with a very quiet manner.

Bernbach's personality had just as much impact on Abbott as his creative skills.

> My natural inclination, being a child of the fifties, was to dress smartly. I had a mother who always told me to wear a suit if I was going for an interview. So I always dressed like Bill Bernbach and, in retrospect, I found it quite useful. I had a Volkswagen client who used to say that I walked into meetings dressed like a banker and pulled all of these wild ideas out to show them. It wasn't a ploy, it was just the way I was and still am.

In an era of uncouth hippies, long-haired pseudo-socialists, drunks, womanisers and n'er-do-wells, David Abbott was an unusual figure. His companions during advertising's boom era tended to loudly announce their assault on advertising's quaint traditions, but Abbott was more stealthy. With his neatly cut fair hair, sober suits and middle-class vowels he didn't fit the wild adman template. Raised in the suburbs of London, son of the owner of a general outfitters shop in Shepherd's Bush, Abbott went from grammar school to study history at Oxford but dropped out after his father died. After running the shops for a short time, he worked his way up from the in-house advertising department at Kodak to Mather and Crowther and eventually DDB's London office. His steady rise to the top was characterised by a studious professionalism and a style of writing that was considered unique. 'David Abbott wrote in this brilliantly simplistic style,' says Frank Lowe. 'Along with John Webster, he was one of only two creatives we wanted at CDP but couldn't get.'

Abbott's sole career ambition had always been to work for Doyle Dane Bernbach. Having become their managing director while still in his twenties, he was aware of a sense that he had peaked too early. Eventually, he resolved to form his own agency because: 'There was no sign of DDB ever making me more than a salaried employee and starting an agency seemed like something I should do at some point.' French Gold Abbott was formed with Mike Gold and Richard French. Throughout the seventies, it grew slowly into a credible agency respected for its creative output. While there he produced high-profile campaigns for Volvo, Terry's Chocolate Orange and Chewits – but he was frustrated. While his more boisterous contempories stole the headlines (and the bulk of the awards) at CDP, BMP and Saatchi & Saatchi, Abbott felt as if he had fallen behind. A merger with a larger agency in the mid-seventies further inhibited Abbott's ambitions. 'As the agency got bigger, we got more desperate to hold on to the clients we had. I found myself having to pitch for business that we already had.' Unhappy, Abbott decided to leave the agency in 1977 – convinced that it was impossible for a large agency to maintain creative credibility. 'I wanted to enjoy writing advertising again,' he says. 'I thought that meant me being in charge of a small agency that only ever had six clients.' It was with these romantic notions that Abbott started an agency that would eventually become the biggest in the UK.

Adrian Vickers was an old friend of Abbott's from Oxford University; Peter Meade was a fellow Millwall fan with whom he would occasionally visit the Den. After the internal conflicts that had beset his time at FGA, Abbott was pleased to form a new agency with close friends. It was an immediate success, driven by Abbott's elegantly written press advertisements. A 1984 ad for Cow and Gate baby food pictured a baby feeding from its mother's breast beneath the headline 'May we recommend the liver and bacon to follow?' With its lengthy passages of explanatory text and sober layout, the advertisement looked like a throwback to a bygone era. Abbott was an advertising anomaly both in personality and creative style: while other agencies were scooping awards for increasingly flashy TV campaigns, Abbott Meade Vickers was producing verbose, thoughtful print ads. But such was the powerful nature of Abbott's writing that the ad received a Gold Award from D&AD. Similarly refined press advertisements for Sainsbury's followed: 'A fickle fungus makes these wines remarkable,' wrote Abbott in reference to the shop's own-label wine. When Sainsbury's started selling their own range of make-up, he conjured the line: 'Pick up a peaches and cream complexion where you pick up your peaches and cream.' Supermarket advertising had traditionally been aimed at working-class housewives with the emphasis on low prices; Abbott's work was credited with single-handedly reshaping the supermarket's image, rendering it the first choice of bourgeois Britain.

All that Abbott Meade Vickers seemed to lack was a flair for television commercials. The rest of the industry suggested that Abbott's pseudo-literary style couldn't be applied to dialogue-driven scripts. But in 1984 he embarked upon a campaign that would swiftly defy such accusations. Yellow Pages wanted to promote the idea that their directory was good for more than just finding plumbers. In an early commercial, Abbott wrote the tale of a septuagenarian scouring local bookshops for a book called *Fly Fishing* by J.R. Hartley. Eventually, he finds a copy of the book with the help of the Yellow Pages – and we discover that he is in fact the author. To film the warm and whimsical story, Abbott chose Bob Brooks. 'Being an American advertiser I was never afraid to make commercials with a high emotional content,' says Brooks.

> When I first came to the UK I found that the ads were funny but there was a reluctance to get too emotional. David Abbott never had that reluctance – he wrote stories that were touching with believable characters. There's nothing wrong with sentiment – why do you think there are so many dogs and babies in commercials? Because the consumer responds to it!

Not everyone agreed. Many among the cynical advertising milieu condemned it as corny. Certainly, it went against the creative grain of the times. With its simplistic story and rose-tinted depiction of small-town Britain, it resembled the best of early seventies television ads. 'It represented great storytelling,' says Brooks. 'At that time, ads were becoming increasingly influenced by the quick-cutting style of MTV. A lot of people liked it and a lot of people hated it – but everyone had a big reaction to it.' The tale had enough resonance to prompt a publisher to produce an actual book called *Fly Fishing* by J.R. Hartley in time for Christmas. 'Can you imagine that?' asks Brooks. 'A fucking book about fishing from an ad!'

The campaign continued throughout the decade, playing on similarly touching tales of everyday life. A father succumbs to his son's requests for a racing bike; a son gets old film footage of his departed father transferred to videotape for his elderly mother. Each commercial went directly for the heartstrings and reflected the unashamedly genteel nature of its creator. 'David was cool and unassuming,' says Brooks. 'He never went in for hyperbole or superlatives. He didn't scream and shout about himself, which was unusual during that era. As a result, he wasn't always talked about as much as many creative directors who weren't as good.'

Abbott's placidity wasn't reflected only in his creative work. In an industry increasingly defined by greedy and aggressive business practice, Abbott Meade Vickers endeavoured to challenge the trend. When they went public in 1986, workers at all levels of the agency owned around thirty per cent of the shares. In the rush to cash in on stock market deregulation, the management of most agencies had kept the bulk of valuable shares in their own hands. While the rest of the industry rode the gravy train, AMV were eyed with a mixture of suspicion and amusement. 'We were referred to in *Campaign* as a bunch of sixties liberals as if it was an insult,' says Abbott.

But I was proud of being a sixties liberal. I don't know what the internal motivations were at Saatchi's but, from the outside, the pitch to buy banks made people realise how out of touch they were with their own capabilities. The eighties was a time in which

191

advertising people perhaps thought they were more important than they really were. We tried to pursue a much quieter course.

Abbott's unhappy time at FGA in the seventies informed his endeavours to make AMV a 'humane and kindly place to work'. The advertising industry had become renowned as a cut-throat environment in which merciless sackings took place as frequently as big-money appointments. In the eyes of the wider business world, it was classed as slipshod and unprofessional. As the eighties unfolded, the image of the champagne-swilling adman living off an expense account grew apace. The accuracy of this stereotype varied from one agency to another but Abbott Meade Vickers were not the only ones trying to dispel the myth.

'Look up the word yuppie in the dictionary and it says "Saatchi & Saatchi" under the definition,' says Dave Trott.

In the eighties, Saatchi & Saatchi gloried in that whole image of dishing out Ferraris and doing lines of coke that went right down the block. Everybody in the industry was doing drugs, admittedly. But the whole yuppie thing of being immensely proud of your Ferrari, your Rolex, your Hermès tie and your suit that cost more than most people's cars – that was mainly going on at Saatchi's.

Dave Trott had been a self-confessed hellraiser during his time at Boase Massimi Pollitt. But when he started his own agency in 1980, he would instil a more robust work ethic.

An imposing and intense individual with enormous self-belief and a booming cockney accent, Trott had spent his formative years working in the shadow of John Webster at BMP. 'I thought I'd be working at BMP for ever,' he says. 'But when John moved up to board level they promoted someone over me to be the creative director. I was happy working for John but wouldn't accept taking orders from anyone else so I left.' His departure coincided with the late-seventies break-up of French Gold Abbott, presenting Trott with an opportunity. 'I thought that no one would give me a creative director's job at a good agency because they didn't know me – John was the star at BMP,' he says.

So I wondered how I could get famous enough to be offered a top job very quickly. I saw that FGA had broken up and David Abbott had formed a new agency. I realised that if I could get either French or Gold to start a new agency with me, people would see my name in *Campaign* alongside that of David Abbott's ex-partner. Suddenly, I'd be boosted up to almost the level of David Abbott in people's minds. So I called up Mike Gold and that's what we did.

Gold Greenless Trott was formed with a distinctive approach to recruitment. 'I could see a lot of agencies wasting huge sums of money on attracting heavyweight creatives who would write one good ad and then goof off,' says Trott. 'But I could take the same money and hire five or six students straight out of college, make them work flat out and get better work out of them in the long run.' Trott's stringent management techniques became the stuff of legend. 'I was like the trainer in the film *Rocky*,' he observes. 'I would say: "Here's how it is: I can tell you what you need to be the best but what I ain't going to do is come round and get you out of bed in the morning to do your run. I'll be out there at seven o'clock and if you're not there then we're not doing this. Let's see how bad you want to be the best."' Trott tried to instil a new generation of admen with the same enthusiasm his peers had felt in the sixties. 'I'd come into our offices in Soho at the weekend and these young kids would be in there working,' he says.

I didn't need to have a feudal approach where I'd whip them if they didn't work hard enough. I said to them, 'You don't have to do jobs you hate like your dads used to. Your work is your hobby. What else are you going to do that's more fun? Go down the pub? Watch TV? Or come into the office and write something that will make you laugh your socks off and that someone will then put four million pounds behind to make it run on the telly? And you're doing it here among young, good-looking, intelligent people in great surroundings.

When GGT were commissioned to produce a series of topical posters advertising London Weekend Television's current affairs output, Trott insisted that his creative staff work on them outside of office hours: 'I said, "If you want to do LWT posters, you do them on your own time – I don't want to see anyone working on them between nine and five." They'd all come in at the weekend because they knew that getting one right would make them famous in the industry very quickly.' The results earned GGT a Silver Award from D&AD in 1982. Over one hundred posters were eventually produced for the campaign, playing on a brand of topical satire made popular by the magazine *Private Eye*. 'At 12 noon on Sunday, Margaret Thatcher talks about her policy on money. (You remember money),' read one particularly striking example. Another showed the shadow of a dangling corpse behind the image of Iranian despot Ayatollah Khomeini. 'He's saving people from choosing the wrong religion,' read the headline.

Meanwhile, Trott was applying his own distinctive style of dialogue to a new type of television commercial. Having spent much of the sixties studying advertising in New York, he had been enamoured with the colloquial style employed by their top ad makers. 'It was all based on New York Jewish humour and dialect,' he says.

When I got back to England I thought, Great, we can do the same thing here using cockney. There's a distinctive humour and language spoken by eight million people in the UK that hadn't been tapped into which I thought was a fantastic opportunity. But at the time all the London agencies were trying to copy New York too directly. They were trying to use that Jewish humour which didn't apply over here.

Hailing from the East End of London, Trott used his own cockney dialogue in an improbable campaign for Toshiba home electricals in which an animated humanoid barked the catchphrase 'Hello Tosh, gotta Toshiba?' Based on the hit single 'Hello John Gotta New Motor?' by comedian Alexei Sayle, it was one of the many eighties jingles to pass into the everyday vernacular. Equally popular was a campaign for Holsten Pils devised by two of Trott's hard-working, underpaid acolytes: Steve Henry and Axel Chaldecott. The series of commercials transposed the comedian Griff Rhys-Jones into scenes from vintage black-and-white movies starring the likes of Humphrey Bogart and Marilyn Monroe. The comedian's own words, which espoused the virtues of the bottled beer, were cleverly edited into the original film dialogue. The ads were some of the decade's most popular and successful, winning a gold award at D&AD and enabling Holsten to acquire a two-thirds share of the Pils lager market. This failed to distract from the fact that the idea was closely based on the Steve Martin film *Dead Men Don't Wear Plaid*. 'They call it a homage but that's a polite way of putting it,' says Trott. 'It was a direct lift.'

Beyond the charm of David Abbott's advertising and the raucous humour Dave Trott lent to the commercial break, the defining theme of eighties advertising was the scramble among advertisers to attach a sense of 'cool' to their brands. No other agency achieved this with greater effect than Bartle Bogle Hegarty. Since the sixties, John Hegarty had been at the forefront of advertising's creative transformation. At Benton and Bowles he had been so passionate about improving creativity he had been fired for 'being a pain in the arse'. But he was not a firebrand in the mould of his colleagues Charles Saatchi or Alan Parker. Hegarty was a small, lean and fair-haired figure who fused his determination ('I was one of the first to ask my employers why the ads had to be so shit') with a distractingly affable manner. .

He was a leading member of Saatchi & Saatchi's successful launch team in the early seventies. From there, he joined the French agency TBWA as the creative director of its London office. Despite some creative success, Hegerty grew dissatisfied with the management structure. 'It was a pan-European agency and it was run along the same lines of socialism,' he says.

Like socialism, it didn't work. The company was part owned by everyone who worked there. Partners at each of their European offices would get a share of profits regardless of their own personal performances. So offices in Frankfurt would be under-performing but earning money because we were doing well. By the early eighties, me and a couple of the other London partners went to the board and said, 'This isn't working – we want a bigger share in our own office's profits.' But they told us to fuck off. So we did.

In 1982, he formed Bartle Bogle Hegerty with John Bartle and Nigel Bogle. With a small team in a one-room office in Soho, they quickly acquired a number of major clients including Audi, Whitbread beer and Levi jeans. Hegerty's approach to each was informed by a cultural shift he saw taking place. 'The 1970s had such a dowdy feel about them,' he says.

It was partly to do with the economic and political climate. But also, punk had told us that being unfashionable was, in fact, fashionable. That was slightly confusing to a lot of people and eventually became wearisome too. In the early eighties I saw a reaction against that. Thatcherism represented a release. Whether you liked it or not, it gave people confidence to show their wealth: to wear that suit, to drive that car, to drink that drink. I think there was an ethos developing in Britain of 'It's not only what you are but how you look that matters'.

The Levi's account presented a particular challenge to BBH. The American jeans brand was considered old fashioned and dull. The fact that it was still a recognisable brand was a further hindrance: the brandishing of designer labels was in conflict with punk's DIY ethos. Furthermore, they were decidedly American during a time when US cultural influences were sneered at in the UK. 'America in the eighties was not admired,' say Hegerty. 'There was Reagan and Iran; its music and fashion wasn't considered cool by young people. So all the things that Levi's was built on were faltering. The heritage of the brand was no longer credible.'

Levi's told Hegerty: 'We need advertising that we will hate.' But Hegerty questioned the brief: 'They thought that anything they liked would automatically be wrong. We didn't buy that idea. We said that when a brand is faltering, you've got to go back to its roots. You just have to find a new way of speaking to people about the core facets of the brand. In Levi's case, that seemed to be the tough way they were built.'

Early commercials centred on the rugged nature of the jeans. Tony Scott was hired to direct 'Stitching', a cinematic pastiche of Steven Spielberg's *Jaws*. Shot in the Gulf of Mexico, it founded on a fisherman's struggle to reel in a marlin – with his tough pair of Levi's proving the decisive factor. Scott, renowned for his love of extreme filming conditions, actually attempted to catch a marlin for the sake of the shoot. 'It was a real challenge to film this marlin while keeping control of the cameras,' says the director. 'Once you get those things on a line they swim at about sixty miles per hour and don't bloody stop. We had cameras on the deck of the boat and three underwater cameras too. It was great.' The resulting commercial was visually stunning. 'There's stitching and there's Levi's stitching,' went the end line.

The ads were critically acclaimed but Levi's were still struggling to be seen as fashionable among young people. When, in 1984, the company decided to relaunch its classic 501 design, it faced further problems. '501s had completely disappeared in the seventies when jeans had become either much wider or much narrower,' says Hegerty. 'But Levi's were coming round to this idea of looking into their back catalogue.'

The slim-cut, five-button 501s with their unusual button flies seemed like a throwback to 1950s Americana. But Hegerty decided to turn this apparent flaw into an asset. 'We realised that the only way you could talk about America in a positive way was to focus on a time when it was still considered cool,' he says. 'The late fifties was its golden age, when it was the driving force of music, fashion and youth culture. The iconography of that period still had a strong resonance.'

Hegerty saw the clean, stylish look of fifties teens (defined by white T-shirts and blue jeans) as being a credible alternative to the scruffiness endorsed by punk. 'We'd noticed the gradual return of a mass fashion look,' he says. '[The pop group] Wham! were becoming very successful with a very slick look. Also, the body beautiful was back in fashion. So we started to piece together this heavily stylised notion of fifties Americana which we thought we could make fashionable.'

The upshot was 'Launderette', which Hegerty devised with copywriter Barbara Nokes. To the tune of Marvin Gaye's 'I Heard It through the Grapevine', a brooding young man walks into a busy launderette in small-town America, *circa* 1958. To the amazement of onlookers, he calmly undresses down to his boxer shorts, throws his jeans into the machine and sits down to read a magazine with a sly grin. The ad ended with the line: 'Levi's 501 – The Original Shrink To Fit Jean'.

The ad seemed to say so little but its impact was immense. To those within the industry it seemed revelatory: it had no dialogue, no explicitly worded brand message, was wilfully nostalgic and yet simultaneously glamorous. The casting of a classically beautiful model defied the 'realistic' casting conventions that had been voguish for much of the previous decade. The soundtrack-led narrative rendered the commercial much closer to an MTV video than anything else in the ad break. The attention paid to authentic detail by director Roger Lyons lent it a captivatingly cool atmosphere. 'Roger wasn't the most fashionable director of the time but I thought he was fantastic,' says Hegerty. 'What we didn't want was a seasoned ad director making what looked like a typical piece of advertising. We wanted something that felt like a little piece of film in itself – something that wouldn't look like the rest of the ad break.' But the sense of authenticity was a ruse: the scene had been created in a west London studio. 'It worked out that way because it had that "shot in front of a live studio audience" American TV show feel to it,' says Hegerty.

'Launderette's immediate success was to reverse the sales decline of Levi's and quickly make them the biggest selling jeans in the market. But the commercial had a much wider impact on the culture of mid-eighties Britain. 'The look we established in that ad had a huge knock-on effect,' says Hegerty. 'Fashion editorial picked it up and soon there was a huge move in that direction. The style became very fashionable and other products like Brylcreem tried to cash in on the same idea of utilising 1950s American iconography.'

The star of the commercial, Nick Kamen, went on to enjoy a fleeting pop music career in the years that followed. Such was the influence of the advertisement, even Kamen's underwear was rendered fashionable. 'Originally, we had scripted the ad so he'd be wearing ordinary Y-fronts under his jeans,' says Hegerty.

But the regulators objected, saying that it wouldn't leave much to the imagination. So we asked them if boxer shorts would be OK and they said yes. Boxer shorts were a long-forgotten, strange sort of undergarment that most young people of the time hadn't even heard of. But once he took off his jeans and revealed them, boxer short sales increased even more than those of Levi's.

Meanwhile, in an early example of what would become known as integrated marketing, Marvin Gaye's record was re-released with the Levi's logo featuring prominently on the sleeve. It went straight into the top ten, as a new generation discovered the appeal of classic Motown records. The campaign would continue well into the following decade using a similarly successful formula of vintage soul music, good-looking models and retro styling. 'We got heavily criticised by the music industry for plundering all these old songs instead of using new stuff in the campaign,' says Hegerty. 'But what they didn't realise was that we were giving rock 'n' roll a history. During the punk era there had been a sense that any music that had gone before was rubbish. But what our ads helped do was introduce young people to all the great stuff that was the roots of modern music.'

Bartle Bogle Hegerty embodied a moody brand of eighties cool. 'We were labelled the lifestyle agency,' says Hegerty.

> It was rumoured that everyone wore black at BBH and there was hair gel in the toilets. A lot of that was crap but we were very stylish because that's what our clients came to us expecting. Audi needed some style injected into their brand. Soon K Shoes and Speedo came to us wanting some of the same sense of style we'd applied to Levi's. At first we didn't like being pigeonholed as the style agency but in the end we thought, Why fight it? It was attracting loads of work.

The Levi's campaign marked a changing cultural landscape in Britain and the beginning of a new era for the advertising industry. Wealth and image were the preoccupations of the eighties consumer; aspirations were raised above those of the sixties and seventies in which gentle, witty adverts surrounding everyday folk were the mainstay of the commercial break. These changing public attitudes may have been driven by socio-economic trends but advertising was quick to respond. 'Advertising doesn't create trends – it just sells into what already exists,' says Dave Trott on reflection. 'If the mood in Britain changed in the eighties to everyone wanting to be yuppies, we responded my making ads about being a yuppie.'

The nuclear families that formed the cast of so many frozen food and packaged goods commercials were an increasingly rare feature of real life in 1980s Britain. Television, music and fashion increasingly fell under the influence of America. Britain seemed a less parochial place, with people looking beyond the confines of tired, little-Britain stereotypes for their cultural guidance. The pioneers of the sixties and seventies had written commercials about a time and place that seemed increasingly outmoded.

As multinational companies expanded across the globe, they wanted advertisers to expand with them. International brands needed international marketing strategies that could translate across national borders. The clever nuance and witty detail of the Hamlet, Heineken, Smash or Yellow Pages commercials were no longer viable for most major brands. John Hegerty's Levi's commercial had set the template for future adverts: broad concepts with flashy visuals, catchy soundtracks and simplistic messages that could appeal equally to viewers in Sweden, America and France. Simultaneously, the power was slowly slipping away from the creative figures who had successfully overhauled the way in which ads were made. Gone were the days when privately owned agencies like CDP could defy the will of clients, flout market research and produce ideas based purely on instinct. By the end of the eighties, most sizeable agencies were public companies with shareholders to answer to. Advertising's rapid growth had led to an excess of agencies all fighting over the same number of clients. In such a climate, advertisers could hardly afford to be as bold in their approach. Instead, they were increasingly forced to pander to a new breed of powerful clients. Many of the creative pioneers left the industry, unable or unwilling to adapt to the changing dynamics. Advertising had become more businesslike and less instinctive. But, to Hegerty, the legacy of his generation of admen lived on. 'Yes, advertising changed after the eighties,' he says.

The creative methods we used in the sixties and seventies couldn't survive because the industry became more businesslike. But the creative principles remained. When we first joined the industry, the work we were doing was absolute crap. There were no principles in it. No one ever told us how advertising should work. It took Bill Bernbach to show us that advertising should be a simple idea dramatically expressed. That it should capture the consumer's attention, involve them and engage them. People say, 'You can't have realised the significance of what you were doing at the time.' But the truth is we did know. We really did feel that we were taking on the old guard and changing the face of advertising for ever.

Epilogue

'How Are You?'

It's 2005 and Frank Lowe is on the other end of the phone, speaking from his house in the south of France. He sounds like the model of the happily retired executive. He fondly recalls the days when he ran the agency that bestrode the advertising world. 'They were great times but it's all about money now. The bad guys moved in and made it all that way. The whole business is about chasing clients and doing whatever they want. I lost interest. I don't need vast amounts of money. I have enough to live in a nice home, play golf when I want, go out for lunch. I'm happy to just sit and talk about the work that I've been involved with in the past.'

After he left CDP, he founded Lowe Howard-Spink and built it into one of the most successful agencies of the 1980s. In 1990, he sold to the American company Interpublic and, backed by their considerable funds, bought numerous agencies around the world which were branded 'Lowe'. By now, Frank was living in Gstaad and commuting to Lowe's New York HQ, often via Concorde. Meanwhile, he pursued high-profile outside interests, serving as president and organiser of the yearly Stella Artois tennis tournament in London. In 1989, he proposed that Interpublic purchase his beloved Manchester United for a price of £15 million. A board member of the American company vetoed the idea, insisting that 'no one watches soccer'.

Eventually, Frank's ways clashed with the formal, fusty processes that controlled Interpublic. In 2003, two years after being knighted, he retired and found a new life as a philanthropist. The man once renowned for his ruthless entrepreneurialism donated £2 million to a city academy school in north London. Now he splits his time between London and France. Right now, there's a mini-reunion taking place near his holiday home. 'My friend Peter Mayle is just down the road,' says Lowe. 'He's shooting a film with Ridley Scott. It's just like old times.'

In the early part of the twenty-first century, the urgent and passionate young men who had once revolutionised British advertising were pursuing quite different lives in a sleepy corner of southern France. While Frank Lowe enjoyed the lazy trappings of retirement, Ridley Scott was taking time out from his busy schedule of making blockbusters to shoot a low-key movie about wine-making with his old adland pal, Peter Mayle. Mayle had quit the advertising industry in 1975 and emigrated to Provence with Jennie Armstrong, who gave up her successful production company to join him. Mayle became a writer and, in 1990, published the international bestseller *A Year in Provence*, which was translated into seventeen languages. The book documented his new idyllic lifestyle – quite the opposite of his wild times at the helm of Papert Koenig and Lois. 'I remember the fantastic D&AD dinners where people would throw bottles of Bollinger at each other,' he says, reclining in the comfort of his country home. 'These days they'd be too worried about getting their frocks dirty.' Not that Mayle misses the hellraising. 'Advertising is a great first job,' he surmises. 'It's fun, you learn a lot and you're well paid. But the greatest talent of those who succeed is knowing when to get out.'

The unique climate in which Mayle and his peers dominated the advertising industry couldn't last for ever. It was a brief time in which social, economic, cultural and political factors all aligned, allowing an incongruous group of individuals to cut a flamboyant swath through a once dull industry. 'It was an atypical era,' says Jeremy Bullmore, who worked in the industry before, during and after the creative revolution took place. As creative head, then chairman, of JWT he represented the establishment the sixties generation opposed. These days, he is a seventy-seven-year-old director of Martin Sorrell's WPP group. At their smart offices in the heart of London's Mayfair, Bullmore sits with his feet on the desk and observes: 'It was an era defined by television. Television is a medium that has totally coloured the way everyone thinks about advertising. But it didn't exist until 1955 and is now under real threat as an advertising medium. But during the so-called creative revolution, one television channel could command twenty million viewers at any given time.'

With such a huge and captive audience, it's understandable that the admen of the sixties, seventies and eighties occasionally got carried away with themselves. Drunken whims that were doodles on a napkin on Monday lunchtime would often be mini-epics broadcast to millions by Saturday evening. Twenty-one-year-olds who were paid more than the prime minister in return for writing rudimentary rhyming couplets were never likely to keep their feet on the ground. Most of them had fallen into the industry by chance. In many cases, they made their way to the top through force of will and a rebellious swagger. Perhaps they were just lucky to have ridden on the gravy train for as long as it lasted. It would be easy to suggest that the characters in this story benefited from being in the right place at the right time: that their only talent was having the chutzpah to grasp the opportunities that came their way. But the fact that so many of them went on to succeed in other fields suggests otherwise. Most of them achieved so much at such a young age that there was still time to build secondary careers in film, publishing, art or politics. The creative revolution might not have happened had the social, cultural and economic circumstances not been in place; without this unique group of individuals, it definitely wouldn't have happened.

It's February 2006 and Sir Frank Lowe is back in Chelsea. He's changed his mind about advertising, given up the easy life in France and, aged sixty-four, started a new agency. His first move was to poach Tesco, the UK's biggest advertiser, from the clutches of his old company, Interpublic. They should have known better than to mess with Frank. At his spectacular home (an old dairy to which he added a French-looking hotel exterior) his tiny dog Lizzy scampers about his feet and underlings pester him with forms to sign and questions to answer – but little seems to penetrate his relaxed demeanour. Until his mobile phone starts to make peculiar noises. 'My telephone keeps asking me, "How are you?" ' he barks. 'It's insulting. I feel like calling up the head of Vodafone and telling him to fuck off!'

With his new company, he hopes to bring a touch of elan back to advertising. 'These huge advertising groups that own hundreds of agencies ruined it for a lot of people,' he says. 'Because of their size, they can afford to charge tiny commissions in order to undercut their rivals. Agencies get so desperate for business that they start pandering to clients. Which is never likely to produce the best creative work.' This was a lesson he learnt in his later years with Interpublic. Now more than ever, says Frank, clients are tricky to deal with. Multinational conglomerates with immense financial power are staffed by marketing directors with degrees, research dossiers and, worst, creative opinions of their own. 'Some of those people are idiots and would probably be better off working in another business!" '

Alan Parker graduated from making kitchen-based ads for frozen foods to directing international hits such as *Midnight Express*, *Evita* and *The Commitments*. In 2002, he was knighted. His offices still sit in Soho, the heart of London's advertising community. 'Ads got too expensive and eventually imploded,' he says. 'It's the same in Hollywood: you can make a fifteen-million-dollar film and no one will bother you. But if you need an eighty-million-dollar budget, the studio executives will be there every day on set. The moment commercials started to be so elaborate, the clients started interfering. Most of the best ads we made in the seventies were simple, cheap and filmed in the basement at CDP.'

When Sir Ridley Scott calls from Los Angeles, he's just learned of the death of one of his former advertising colleagues. 'He was only my age but he had a heart attack,' he laments. 'It just goes to show: you've got to find a ball you like bouncing and try to do it a few times a week. Personally, I like tennis. I'm good at it too. I mean, I'm very good. I play with pros.' Frank Lowe can verify: 'I played Ridley at Queens Club once,' he says. 'It was one set all when I fell and twisted my ankle. It blew up immediately like a balloon and I said, "Ridley, this is awful, I'm going to have to go inside." And he looked and it and said, "Can't we just finish the third set?"'

Scott carried his tenacity and competitiveness into Hollywood, making a series of blockbusters including *Alien*, *Blade Runner*, *Thelma and Louise* and *Gladiator*. Unlike many of his contemporaries, he always kept a hand in advertising. Ridley Scott Associates remains one of the world's busiest advertising production companies. 'I still look at showreels every week to scout new talent,' he says. And he's still available for advertising projects himself, given the right conditions. 'It's more complicated these days,' he says.

I shot 'Border Crossing' for Benson and Hedges in a day and had it edited by the end of the week. An ad of that scale nowadays would take five months of people sitting around talking about it before it even got close to being shot. The problem these days is everyone and their mother wants to have a say in how the ad is made. I'm bemused by it. Back then, people were willing to let you get on with it. They trusted you and were excited to see what you might do with the commercial. Then it changed and became an atmosphere whereby you had to go into a room full of people at an ad agency and prove to them why you were a genius before they'd even consider you for the script. My attitude to that kind of thing was: 'Next!'

Despite his busy film-making schedule, Ridley Scott finds time to monitor his commercials company, which still thrives in Soho. 'My brother is a fucking maniac!' says Tony Scott. 'He'll be in the middle of a major production with Russell Crowe and Denzel Washington but every day he's on the phone to RSA in London. We both like to keep a strong hand in the company – we love the business side of things.'

The younger of the Scott brothers continues to specialise in the slickest and most spectacular of Hollywood movies, having followed his early successes with critically acclaimed hits such as *True Romance* and *Crimson Tide*. He's saddened by the apparent reluctance among modern agencies to hand him and Ridley more adverts. 'We are the godfathers of the industry and so I suppose we intimidate people,' he says. 'Still, a little bit of intimidation is good. Our reputations go before us. I fucking hope so anyway!'

Sid Roberson continued to be one of Britain's top commercial directors throughout the eighties and nineties. But he never lost the snarling defiance that had characterised his early career. 'I was on a set in the nineties where twenty-one clients turned up and each of them wanted a say on every single shot,' he says. 'In the end I said, "Look, here's what I'm gonna do. I'll sit you all in three rows of seven and give each of you a set of cards marked one to ten like in the Olympics. After each shot, I want you to remain silent and hold up your cards. If it averages five or more, I'll make it a print."'

There were few tempers to compare with that of Bob Brooks in his directing heyday. But in contrast to Scott and Roberson, Brooks appears to have mellowed with age. He splits his time between France, Japan and London. He lectures to students on advertising. 'I tell them that the backbone of British advertising in its heyday was storytelling,' he says.

> Most of the commercials had nothing to do with effects. Even when Hugh [Hudson] filmed 'Swimming Pool' for Benson and Hedges, the impact was extraordinary but there was nothing added to the commercial in post-production. Everything you saw on screen was exactly as Hugh had captured it on camera. In the post-MTV era, fast cutting and special effects began to take the place of proper storytelling.

'The older I get the more I realise that each generation lives and dies and no one's around to remember what happened previously. So the next generation has to start all over again,' says Dave Trott, still the creative director of his own advertising agency in 2006.

> All of the new generation's ads looks exactly like the kind of nonsensical 1950s crap we were trying to get the fuck away from. There's an advert out at the moment for a mobile phone network featuring two Chinese cowboys and a jellyfish. There's people going around saying, 'It's so bad, it's good!' No! It's so bad, it's bad! The whole process is run by know-nothing fuckwits at the client's end and know-nothing fuckwits in the planning department of agencies, all of whom have done their marketing courses and are armed with strategies. But none of it has anything to do with finding a logical way to speak to the punter. Which is what creatives used to do.

In December 2005 John Webster is seventy-one years old, lean, fit-looking and still based in the Paddington office where he invented the Smash Martians, the Cresta Bear and the Honeymonster. The walls are still covered by an eclectic mix of newspaper and magazine cuttings. 'There is a danger,' he says. 'That advertising won't attract the best people any more because it feels less creative and more corporate and dull.' Webster was never bothered by the input of planners or research. But the creative process eventually became troublesome even for him. 'These days we're advertising products with the same campaign all over the world,' he says. 'You might just be able to convince your client in England that your idea is funny – and even that's harder to do these days – but then you have to convince a guy in Japan, Kenya and South America too.' In January 2006 John Webster died of a heart attack while jogging near his home in Hertfordshire.

Webster's legacy, along with those of Bill Bernbach, who died in 1982, and Colin Millward, who died in 2004, still lives on in the ad break, says David Abbott. 'The principles remain the same as they did back then,' he says. 'At the good agencies they still conform to the same truths we were fighting for in the sixties, which were: find something relevant to say about your product and say it in a way that can't be missed.' Abbott is retired and writing a book. Unlike may of his peers, he still finds the commercial break quite exciting.

I saw an ad for the iPod which was just a silhouette of someone dancing to some music. The idea might be for the product to look like the most modern thing there is – and that's what it achieved without any words at all. Doing the common thing uncommonly well remains the nub of successful selling just as it was back in the old days. You might now do it in new mediums but it's not the delivery that matters. Only the idea.

Lord Tim Bell stands in the centre of his top-floor office at Chime Communications, chain-smoking Dunhill cigarettes. His company is the UK's number-one PR firm and encompasses dozens of other communication services. He surveys the Mayfair skyline and laments: 'We used to admire success but now we hate it. We attack it, we criticise those who have it and look for flaws in them.' Following his departure from Saatchi & Saatchi, Bell became a special adviser to Margaret Thatcher and was knighted in 1990. He now purveys

PR advice to, among others, Rupert Murdoch, Ukrainian president Viktor Yuschenko and McDonald's. In 2006, he was advising the Iraqi authorities on how to sell democracy to the populace.

> I was lucky enough to work with the greatest prime minister this country has ever seen and two of the greatest admen as well: Charlie Saatchi and Frank Lowe. I think myself incredibly lucky to have known them, but we won't see their like again. No one is put on a golden pedestal any more. There is an obsession with everyone being equal – no one can be picked out as superior. There used to be people in advertising who possessed genius. If David Abbott had been born in a different era he would have been a romantic poet. He would have been alongside Keats. If you can see that, count yourself bloody lucky that you've been living during the same era as him!

Sir Martin Sorrell is the most powerful advertising executive in the world; he built Wire and Plastic Products, the shell company he bought in 1985, into the world's biggest marketing company. In 2005, it was worth over £5 billion, employed 84,000 staff worldwide and enshrined over one hundred marketing services brands. 'We are a full service company, just like JWT was in the fifties,' he explains. He is small, darts around the room while he talks and continually breaks off his eloquent and passionate diatribe to answer calls. Despite being perhaps the world's busiest man, he responds to an interview request via email within two minutes – quicker than any other person involved with this story. 'People say the industry grew down but I think it grew up like all industries have to. It couldn't go on being artsy-crafty for ever and relying only on people's instincts. Creativity still shines through. There is still room for mavericks.'

For a few years, those mavericks came in from the sidelines and took charge of the industry. In the new advertising world, they have gone back to performing cameo roles while suited businessmen take care of the serious stuff. As a prerequisite for success in advertising, creative flair has been relegated to a lowly position. Sir Martin Sorrell's favourite quote, by Calvin Coolidge, reads:

> Nothing in the world can take the place of persistence. Talent will not; nothing is more common than unsuccessful men with talent. Genius will not; unrewarded genius is almost a problem. Education will not; the world is full of educated derelicts. Persistence and determination alone are omnipotent. The slogan 'press on' has solved and always will solve the problems of the human race.

Charles Saatchi eventually lost interest in advertising and went on to be the world's most influential collector of modern art. In a rare 2006 Q&A in the *Independent* newspaper, a reader emailed him the following: 'Your first wife is on record as saying that she only ever saw you reading comic books. Have you ever actually read a book? And if so, what was it?'

'Are you asking if I'm thick?' Saatchi responded. 'I suppose I am rather, but that doesn't seem to hamper a career in advertising.'

Acknowledgements

Thanks to everyone who agreed to be interviewed, not only for the interviews themselves but for your help and support without which this book couldn't have been written. Thanks also to Carol Cass, David Bernstein and Rob Morris whose words might not have made the final draft but who provided me with invaluable background insight, info and anecdote. And thanks to Kai Hsiung at RSA and Barbara Seymour, both of whom went out of their way to facilitate interviews, dig out numbers and be generally helpful when I'm sure they had better things to do.

Thanks to Mike Wadding, whose brilliant documentary, *The Men from the Agency*, served as an inspiration. And thank you Paul Delaney, who helped me realise I had an idea worth writing about.

Thanks to Theo and Cas for their interest and advice and Sue for all that typing. And to Chris Payne for the typing and everything else over the years. And for their emotional support, Dom and the rest of the secretive GICF.

A colossal thanks to Jocasta Hamilton at Sceptre for giving me the opportunity to write this book and being brilliant in every single way throughout the whole process. I'd also like to thank Phil Hilton for getting me started ten years ago.

Thanks always Bren and Baz, aka my mum and dad.

But most of all: thanks for every single, little thing Anna. I love you.

Bibliography

BERNSTEIN, DAVID: *Creative Advertising*, Suffolk, The Creative Business, 1974

BULLMORE, JEREMY: *More Bull More: Behind the Scenes in Advertising (Mark III)*, Henley-On-Thames, World Advertising Research Centre, 2003

DELLA FEMINA, JERRY: *From Those Wonderful Folks Who Gave You Pearl Harbor*, New York, Pocket Books, 1970

D&AD Annuals, London, D&AD, 1963–1996

FALLON, IVAN: *The Brothers: The Rise and Fall of Saatchi & Saatchi*, London, Hutchinson, 1988

FENDLEY, ALISON: *Saatchi & Saatchi: The Inside Story*, New York, Arcade Publishing, 1995

HIGGINS, DENIS: *The Art of Writing Advertising*, New York, McGraw Hill, 2003

KING, EMILY: *Robert Brownjohn, Sex and Typography*, London, Laurence King Publishing, 2005

MAYLE, PETER: *Up the Agency: The Funny Business of Advertising*, New York, St Martin's Griffin, 1990

MORGAN, KENNETH O: *The Oxford Illustrated History of Britain*, Oxford, Oxford University Press, 1984

MYSERSON, JEREMY & VICKERS, GRAHAM: *Rewind, Forty Years of Design and Advertising*, London, Phaidon, 2002

OGILVY, DAVID: *Confessions of an Advertising Man*, London, Southbank Publishing, 1963

PUGH, MARTIN: *State And Society: A Social and Political History Of Britain*, 1870–1997, London, Arnold, 1994

RITCHIE, JOHN & SALMON, JOHN: *Inside Collett Dickenson Pearce*, London, Batsford, 2000

WELLS LAWRENCE, MARY: *A Big Life (In Advertising)*, New York, Touchstone, 2002